Grace for Grief

A Mother's Journey of Love and Loss

PAM KIRK MCCARTY

Grace for Grief is an incredible memoir that will teach you to be a better human being. When faced with unfathomable tragedy, McCarty takes your hand and guides you through the darkness to find light and love through memory and action. It's a page-turner you may go back to when searching for your own strength.

—Dr. Niles Reddick
Pulitzer Prize-nominated author of *Who's Going to Pray for Me Now?*

Grace for Grief: A Mother's Journey of Love and Loss is a heartfelt memoir that gently walks readers through the realities of love, loss, and healing. With honesty and compassion, McCarty shares her personal journey through grief, offering comfort, understanding, and hope to anyone facing the pain of losing a loved one. This book serves as a reminder that even in sorrow, grace can be found.

—Susannah Lewis
USA Today bestselling author of *Can't Make This Stuff Up*

With honesty and compassion, Pam McCarty honors her daughter Morgan's life while sharing the painful, tender, and ultimately healing journey of grief. For any parent who has lost a child, or anyone seeking comfort and hope after loss, this book offers wisdom, companionship, practical advice, and the reassurance that healing is possible. It is a generous and meaningful gift to all who grieve.

—Debra Landwehr Engle
Author of *The Only Little Prayer You Need*

Having walked the painful journey of sudden grief and loss myself, I deeply connected with the emotions expressed by author Pam McCarty in her debut memoir, *Grace for Grief*. Loss is a universal experience, yet its impact leaves deep and lasting scars on the hearts of those left behind.

Finding the path to forgiveness is a journey all its own, deeply intertwined with grief. It is not easy, and it rarely comes quickly. It requires grace, deep faith, and the courage to pray for healing even when the heart feels shattered.

Grace for Grief gently reminds us that even in our darkest moments, healing is possible.

—Michelle Cowan
Speaker, author of *Better Not Bitter*
Podcaster on *From Loss to Light*
Screenwriter of *Whispers From Heaven*

When a parent grieves, the most meaningful gift is a book that reaches out, holds their sorrow, and reminds them they're not alone. *Grace for Grief* offers that kind of comfort.

—Karen C. McCord
Author of *The Lessons of the Lilies*

This memoir reflects the author's personal experiences and recollections. While every effort has been made to present events truthfully, certain names, identifying details, and circumstances may have been changed to protect the privacy of individuals. Dialogue has been reconstructed from memory, and in some cases individuals or events may be combined for narrative clarity.

ISBN: 979-8-9950380-1-6 (paperback)

ISBN: 979-8-9950380-0-9 (ebook)

Published by Glimmer & Grace

Cover design: Janyre Tromp

Interior design: Janyre Tromp

Publishing services provided by Ember & Vine Press, LLC

Printed in the United States of America

This book is dedicated to my loves,
Mike and Kirk, who lived this journey with me.
You were my anchor in the
present while I visited the past.

1

THE CALL

Darkness sets in; there is no sun.
—Unknown

With tornado sirens blaring and torrents of rain flooding the streets, my husband and I had already experienced a frightful night. It was past eleven o'clock when we were plunged into the worst nightmare of our lives with one phone call, the call no parent wants to receive.

When tornado warnings happen in our city of Jackson, Tennessee, we listen. A mere three years earlier, in 2003, an F4 tornado had decimated the downtown area, ripping through East Jackson and leaving hundreds without homes. North of town, Union University was torn apart, and the city was left with eleven fatalities. Thankfully, the storm had raged through on a Sunday night, when the downtown community was not working. Otherwise, more lives could have been lost.

So, when the shrill tornado sirens sounded on Friday, September 22, 2006, Mike and I rushed to the safety of our basement and remained there until the television weather team assured us the danger had passed. It was a violent storm that extended both before and after the official tornado warnings. In its wake, many shattered windows and downed trees remained. I can still hear the torrential rain beating the house, gushing from our gutters, as hail pounded the windows and the roof.

Only after the winds had died down did we feel safe to come upstairs from the basement. I had just found my nightgown and was brushing my teeth when the phone rang. Assuming it was my sister calling to check on us after the storm, I kept brushing my teeth in the en suite bathroom while Mike answered the phone in our primary bedroom.

"Yes?" exclaimed my husband in an unusually tense tone. "What happened? Is she all right? Where is she?"

Hearing the sheer panic in his voice, I ran out of the bathroom, wringing my hands, asking him to tell me who was on the other end.

He put the phone on speaker so I could hear as a nurse explained that Morgan had been hit by a car and admitted to the University of Tennessee Medical Center. "You need to get here as soon as possible."

With panicked eyes and his voice growing more desperate, Mike nearly shouted into the phone. "What's her condition?"

The nurse responded, "Critical."

"We're on the way," Mike stammered as he collapsed on the bed.

In an isolated moment, I stood frozen and confused. My brain couldn't process the shocking news. "How can this be? I just talked with her a few hours ago, and she was fine."

Tears filled my eyes. "Do you think she'll be all right? I need to talk to the nurse. Call her back."

A return call gave us little more information. We only knew that our daughter was in critical condition in the ICU. Struggling to catch my breath, I grabbed the nearest clothes, threw one set on, and packed more into a bag. In a state of panic, Mike and I dashed about the house getting ready to go.

By now it was 11:30 p.m., and the UT Med Center was nearly a five-hour drive from our home on a clear day. It would likely take longer in bad weather, especially so late at night. We knew several friends with small airplanes, but getting a plane up in tornado weather was out of the question.

Within ten minutes, with overflowing bags stuffed with random clothes, we rushed out into the storm, determined to reach our daughter as soon as possible. Dripping with rain, I jumped in the car completely numb. My fingers were so cold I couldn't feel them, and my nerves were raw.

She's alone. Morgan needs us. She's alone.

Overcome with fear and sadness, my bones physically ached knowing I was so far away from my child in her hour of need. I desperately wanted to be there with her, to soothe her and hold her, but I did not yet know what we would be told when we finally reached the hospital.

I'd talked to Morgan several times earlier that very day. She'd been so excited that it was homecoming weekend at the University of Tennessee in Knoxville, where she had been enjoying her junior year. She was going on a date with a new guy and had even called me halfway into the night to say she was having a great time. She related all the places they'd gone with groups of friends, and she was happy to have run into friends from Jackson too.

Morgan had beamed through the entire conversation. "I can't wait to come home next weekend and see you and Dad." She'd even ended the call, as she usually did, by overwhelming us with, "I love you! We'll talk tomorrow."

Please, God. Don't let that be the last time I hear her voice.

She was having a wonderful time and enjoying life to the fullest. With strong academic grades and a thriving social calendar, she'd made the most of her college experience and even had plans to study abroad in Florence, Italy, her favorite city. This summer was to be the culmination of her dream to return to the country she loved and visited as a teenager. I was comforted to see her doing exactly what she wanted to do with her life. She was content and happy. What more could a mother want? And I was always grateful that we talked two to three times each day, usually as she walked across campus to class. I found such joy in hearing of her escapades, and I was thankful she shared so much with me.

But now, I couldn't reach her. All I wanted was to hear Morgan's voice.

With fingers trembling, I called my sister Donna and burst out the news in a distraught voice.

"We're already on the way to Knoxville," I explained, adding that we'd been given very few details about Morgan's condition. As a nurse, my sister tried to reassure me that this was probably just a minor injury. Still, she was going to be there to support us.

"Oh, my gosh, I'm leaving now and will be right behind you," Donna blurted. "I'll pick up Kirk as I go through Nashville."

Kirk, our older son, was living in Nashville, where he had just started a new job.

"Yes, pick him up." My voice quavered as I thanked her for all her help.

As the minutes passed, I called Donna again and frantically told her to get our other sister, Kandy, as she was driving through Nashville. I had a suspicion I was going to need all the family support I could get.

What if? What if she does not make it? What will we do then? I can't imagine life without our precious Morgan.

Too anxious to wait, I called the hospital again, only to become frustrated when they would not give us any specifics about her condition. Due to their guarded answers, I feared the situation was not good. I glanced at the ceiling of the car, trying to grasp what was happening.

In just a matter of minutes, our lives have been turned upside down.

I started calling a few of my closest friends, asking them to pray for Morgan. Without any idea of what to pray for specifically, I asked God for help and for her to be alive.

Tears shimmered down my cheeks as I stared out at the blurring scenery, trying to make sense of the irrational situation. Why wouldn't the hospital give us any information? My life was breaking into pieces, and my heart had become shattered glass.

Our speeding trip gave Mike and me time to digest what little information we had been given. However, it was also a dangerous four and a half hours for our frantic thoughts. A million things were going through my head, and I'm sure Mike was just as distraught.

Surely, we can stop and rewind to the time when she was safe at home in her apartment.

My mind ran through every possible scenario, and I began to fear the worst.

Almost whispering to Mike, I said, "Injuries heal. We can take her home to recover. If surgery is required, I'll stay as long as it takes to get her well."

Very calmly to myself, I asked God to take Morgan in his arms, and then, for a flash of a second, I thought, should I be mentally planning her services?

No, I am getting too carried away and emotional. This may not be as bad as we believe.

"How much longer do we have?" I asked Mike. The wait was too agonizing. "I want somebody to give us some answers."

This was not supposed to happen to our beautiful, twenty-year-old daughter who had everything ahead of her in life. With dread and numbness growing in the pit of my stomach, Mike broke the speed limit and raced onward through the stormy night.

In the middle of blinding rain, Mike frantically drove into the emergency room parking area, and we rushed inside to be met by a pair of nurses. The whole scene had a charged feeling of anticipation as I fought tears. "Where is she?" I shouted. "I want to see her!"

A nurse took my hand and explained the situation. "Morgan was walking home. She was only a block from her apartment when a car came over the hill. It hit her and kept on going. The young man walking with her called 911, and the ambulance responded right away. She was given medical care and arrived here in less than ten minutes."

I would later learn that Morgan had called her roommates around 10:30 p.m. as she was walking home to share a pizza with them. She'd enjoyed a fun homecoming date and had no awareness that danger was near.

Just one block away. She was so close to being safe at home.

Little did I know that was the last time anyone would hear her voice.

We rushed to the third floor, where we found our precious daughter in a sterile ICU room with a team of doctors surrounding her bed. Despite their somber glances, Morgan looked like she was sleeping peacefully. Although she had monitors attached to her head, not a single scratch could be seen on her. No bruising, not a drop of blood. Her makeup was still perfect, and her long, cascading blond hair spilled over the pillow. She didn't look injured at all. In fact, she looked angelic.

I felt like the whole trip had been a mistake. Morgan was lying in the hospital bed with none of the visible injuries I had imagined during our frantic journey from Jackson. I just knew she would open her eyes and continue the fun homecoming weekend she had planned.

The weekend that was never to happen.

The doctors explained that they had taken several scans and would continue to monitor her for any progress. "Morgan has suffered multiple internal injuries, and her brain activity has been getting weaker and weaker," one doctor said. "Her body is shutting down from injuries to her major organs."

I could not believe what I had heard. Stunned, I questioned the doctors. "Is there anything else that can be done?"

They gave us no hope of recovery.

Shocked and not wanting to believe their dire prognosis, we all erupted into tears. Numbness took over my senses. As the doctors and nurses left us in our grief, we were faced with the realization that Morgan was not going to live through this tragedy.

With tears streaming down my face, I struggled to comprehend the fact that my worst nightmare had come true. Mike and I fell into each other's arms and sobbed.

Even if I walk through a very dark valley,
I will not be afraid,
because you are with me.
Your rod and your shepherd's staff comfort me.
—Psalm 23:4

Soon, my two sisters arrived with our son, Kirk. My heartbroken family did not leave Morgan's crowded room that night, and my husband and I never left her side. Spreading out on the floor, just to be near her, some tried to sleep, but sleep escaped me. Like a ship on rough seas, I was tossed and turned by restless thoughts.

At some point, I glanced at the clock and realized it was now the early hours of Saturday, September 23, 2006. I had been up all night, praying and dreading the morning sun. Now we were entering the final day of Morgan's life. Anger, frustration, and blind numbness came over me as I struggled to accept what the medical team had advised us to do —remove life support.

"Why?" I screamed to God. "Why has this happened to our family?"

Mike and Kirk were inconsolable, as were my sisters. Our entire family clung to each other, hoping to survive this unbearable situation.

In retrospect, that day was tragic and incomprehensible, not only for us, but for hundreds of others who stood vigil outside the doors of the ICU.

One of the nurses came into the room with her hands up and panic in her voice. "What do you want me to do with the crowd of her friends in the waiting room? They're overflowing down the halls of the hospital."

By that time, a group of fifty friends had grown to hundreds, all waiting to know if Morgan would be all right.

I asked the nurse to tell them, "Because of Morgan's severe injuries, the daylong process of removing life support has begun." That process has haunted our thoughts and dreams ever since.

After a short time, the nurse returned. "They aren't leaving. We're overrun with anxious students who are inconsolable and weeping. It's getting so crowded in the hallways. They're sitting on the floor of the lobby, and we have nowhere to put them. Should we send them away?"

But the Lord stayed with me and gave me strength.
—2 Timothy 4:17

My prayers came back as a silent form of stamina that I did not know existed in me. Somehow, God gave me the ability to handle what was coming next. It was as if I had been granted a sudden burst of clarity within my grief-stricken heart, a divine energy that held me up and told me what to do.

"Let them come in, a few at a time, to tell Morgan goodbye," I told the nurse. "Her friends were so important to her. They're hurting too."

2

MY MAN

A flower cannot blossom without sunshine,
and man cannot live without love.
—Max Müller

Years earlier, in 1970, I asked the love of my life to go with me to a high school dance. Or so the story is told by my husband. Nobody seems to remember which of my friends called Mike from the bedroom at Anne's house that day when we were in the tenth grade. You see, for a high school Kappa Chi sorority dance, girls were expected to do the asking. But the way I remember it, I did not even talk to Mike on the phone. My friends made the request for me and, with a yes from Mike, the deal was sealed without a word from me at all. So, I will leave it up to you to decide whose memory is right. Either way, our first date was that Christmas dance when we were teens.

Mike was a handsome six-foot-three with blond hair, deep green eyes, and a shy, quiet demeanor. When this impressive football player showed up at my house the night of the dance, my dad stated only one sentence. "I'm glad she finally got someone tall enough to date."

Up to that point, I'd been in the habit of going to dances with guys who were shorter than my five-foot-six. Now my dad thought I'd hit the jackpot with this tall one. And Dad was right; it proved to be a magical first date.

I wore a short, black-and-white dress with black straps and a big organza bow across the bodice. The sheer, flowing look was complemented by black, strappy sandals and a small, black satin purse with gold wire straps and embedded gemstones.

By the end of the night, my friends were calling for details.

"Not only is he good-looking, but he can dance!" I admitted.

We all knew from experience that boys our age were not only bad dancers, but most of them were not interested in dancing at all. Mike and I danced the night away and had the time of our lives.

We continued dating after that first dance and never stopped.

My sisters adored him, especially my tomboy sister, Kandy, who was glad to finally have a boy around the house to play basketball with her. He always came to our house with a load of sports equipment, which thrilled her athletic soul. She saw him as a big brother, since she was only eight years old when we started dating. Both of my sisters probably drove him crazy by having him run races outside and play any games they could drag out longer. He was always a good sport and learned to love them both. Of course, they idolized him and soaked up as much attention as he could give them.

Mike soon became a fixture at all our family gatherings and holidays, so my whole extended family of cousins, grandparents, aunts, and uncles knew him well and loved him, as I did. My dad was not quick to warm up to any of the guys my sisters and I dated through the years. He also claimed to have a touch of selective memory. Only after a two-year span of Mike spending time at our house did Dad finally call him Mike instead of "that boy." Dad was not sure about anyone dating his daughters. He protectively kept his distance, checking each guy out as a first line of defense.

After seven years of dating, Mike and I were married on March 5, 1977, at Lambuth University Chapel. My dad was glad to finally have a boy in the family, and Dad and Mike formed a tight bond. Dad sold heavy equipment for Road Builders Equipment Company, but on weekends, he would go to help on his farm. A hired farmer would take care of the day-to-day needs. For many years he raised cattle, and other times he leased his land for crops. There were always things to do on the farm, mainly checking on the horses and animals and mending fences. They would go to our family's hobby farm on weekends, where Mike helped Dad with random chores. Dad also took Mike goose hunting to his sacred place in Texas. That was a first for Mike, and the hunting trip proved that Mike was a good addition to our family.

Mike and I always got along well, despite having opposite personalities. I was an outgoing cheerleader who had never met a stranger. Mike was more on the quiet side with a great sense of humor. Somehow, it all worked.

Now that I had graduated from college and married the love of my life, I was ready to begin my teaching career. Because it was spring, I worked as a substitute teacher until the academic year finished. Then I accepted a full-time teaching position in the fall of 1977, while Mike finished his college degree at Lambuth.

Within a year, we had bought our first home together, a nice three-bedroom house in Jackson, Tennessee. During the first five years of our marriage, with no kids at home yet, we traveled with friends and lived a carefree lifestyle. There was never a dull moment, as these were our party years. We enjoyed plenty of summer days at the pool with friends, visiting each other's houses, attending parties, or going to area events. Lots of good memories came from these times, and we established a core group of forever friends.

I was twenty-six when I found out I was expecting our first child, a boy. For my family, it was the first grandchild. For Mike's family, it was the first who would be living in town, so it was an exciting time for all of us. When Donna and I were in junior high, we'd both announced we wanted to name our future son Kirk, since it was our maiden name. I had insisted that since I was the oldest, I would have the first choice. Now it was time to see what Mike had to say about the idea. Thankfully, Mike agreed, and we also selected Michael in honor of my husband.

Two weeks before my due date, our friends hosted a couple's shower for Kirk Michael. I went into labor during the party and was admitted to the hospital. While there, I sent my sisters to launder all the new baby clothes, hoping they'd wash any chemicals out of the fabric. I had been saving that task for last so the clothes would smell fresh and clean for the baby.

When Kandy and Donna arrived at the hospital, they hung an "It's a Boy" banner on my hospital door and brought a blue zip-up suit for Baby Kirk to wear home. Shower guests called the hospital for updates while I was in labor and said the party was still going strong.

When a C-section was deemed necessary, everything moved into high gear. As the surgeon made his cut, Mike, who had been by my side the entire time, became weak in the knees and was escorted to a chair. Soon, Kirk was delivered and was perfect in every way, all seven pounds, eleven ounces of him.

After we arrived home with Kirk, and much to my surprise, I found those newly laundered baby clothes all wadded up in a ball and wrinkled in the dryer. I was grateful Kandy had "helped," so I could only laugh. We were all new to this baby thing, learning as we went along.

Kirk's first word was *Dada*, then *ball*, then *Mama*. At a young age, he could not have enough balls or cars to play with. He could be found *vrooming* around the house with all the Matchbox cars he could carry. A blond, green-eyed carbon copy of his handsome father, Kirk had a quiet side to his personality, like his dad. Besides playing soccer and baseball, he loved to swim, and we spent many days enjoying the southern sunshine for hours at a time.

Three and a half years later, in 1985, I found out I was expecting again, but this time we decided not to learn the sex of the baby. I decided gender didn't matter, as long as the baby was healthy.

Donna, a nurse in labor and delivery at the hospital, peeked at my records and told me she knew the sex. I held off as long as I could, but the curiosity finally got to me. When I finally surrendered, she let me know we were expecting another boy. Soon, I was washing Kirk's baby clothes, leaving his outgrown nursery the same, with no need to redecorate.

During my delivery, Donna was not on duty like she had been with Kirk's birth. Instead, she was in the room as a proud aunt this time. As soon as I heard the doctor say, "It's a girl," the screams of joy and surprise rang to the roof.

We had planned all along for another boy. What happened?

The doctor, a long-term friend, couldn't stop laughing. He confessed he had known it was a girl from the start, but he'd changed the symbol on my chart intentionally. He knew I didn't originally want to know the gender, but he also knew my sister would spill the beans in a weak moment.

After months of thinking my baby was a boy, this was a great surprise, and I thanked the doctor for helping me keep the sex unknown until the birth. Donna, like the rest of us, had been taken in by the joke, but it was a thrill to have a baby girl, and we were all overjoyed.

Now that we had welcomed a girl, my sisters rushed to my hospital room to remove the "It's a Boy" banner they had displayed. They quickly put up an "It's a Girl" sign and gifted me with a pink outfit to take our baby girl home.

Morgan Leah McCarty, named after Donna's middle name, came into this world with an unexpectedness that gave us a moment of happy tears, cheers, and celebration.

The celebration never left her. With golden locks and sea-mist eyes, our newborn daughter illuminated any room.

Mike and I, along with our cherub-faced little Kirk, felt blessed by this special gift. As her parents, we always understood that this gift was far too valuable not to be shared. And it is in the sharing of Morgan's life that we have all been blessed.

Morgan's granddad, Pop, had no idea just how prophetic he would turn out to be when he dubbed his newborn granddaughter, "Pop's Little Princess." Perhaps he was reminded of fairytales, but something about Morgan evoked thoughts of crowns, magic wands, and glass slippers.

She loved taking center stage and was never happy unless we were thoroughly entertained by her presence. Her Aunt Denise can vouch for this. When Morgan was at the tender age of four, her very proud aunt had requested a lunch date at anywhere that Morgan wanted to go. Morgan chose to partake of her favorite delicacy, Wendy's. While her indulgent aunt was ordering lunch, Morgan walked into the dining room and saw the opportunity to perform. Because she had just seen the movie *Dirty Dancing*, she proceeded to leap up onto one of the tables, adjust the straps on her monogrammed jumper, and belt out the famous lyrics to "Do You Love Me (Now That I Can Dance)" by The Contours.

After her stellar performance, she received a standing ovation from the lunchtime crowd, and as they say, "A star was born."

Yes, Morgan was always the happiest when she could make someone else happy too. In fact, according to her college friends, one of her nicknames was Superstar. Her often-performed childhood rendition of "The Star-Spangled Banner," which contained added phrases of how Jesus loved all the little children of the world, is a perfect example of how her little imperfections endeared her to us all. I loved her glow, and more importantly, we loved how she always used her light to brighten our worlds.

As much as my father's aloofness had irritated Mike when we were dating, he ended up doing the same thing years later when Morgan started dating. As the protective daddy bear of his little girl, Mike was not at all friendly to the boys who came to see her. He had a rule not to smile at any of them, preferring to display his cold disapproval. Kirk was right behind him, critiquing all of Morgan's dates. None of them was ever good enough for his little sister.

At one eighth-grade dance, all the parents went to take pictures of the teens in their finery before the party. As Morgan and her date spilled out of the car with other couples, I beamed. "Don't all the young ladies look radiant in their dresses! You guys look sharp too! Let's get in line for pictures. We want to capture this moment."

The whole time, Mike watched from a distance, not saying a word. He did lean over and kiss Morgan gently on the cheek while boasting, "I think you are the loveliest one here."

"Aww! Dad, thanks. You are too sweet. Thanks for coming for the pictures with Mom."

Stoic Mike never cracked a smile at Andrew, Morgan's date, nor at the rest of the young men.

Andrew sidled up to me a few minutes later and bent down to whisper, "Mrs. Pam, I don't think Mr. Mike likes me."

"I'm sure he likes you, Andrew," I assured him as I put my hand on his shoulder. "He's teasing you, and he's being a protective father."

"Okay, I'm glad that's all," said Andrew. "I have sisters too, and I know what that's like with my dad."

A little white lie doesn't count where fatherhood is concerned.

Later that evening, I related the question that Morgan's date had asked me, and Mike said, "No, I don't like him. He's with our daughter, isn't he?"

That tough love shone through, just like it did with my father and my dates.

Yes, Mike and Kirk were a force to be reckoned with. The only problem was that Kirk was usually at the events Morgan attended, so his probing eyes would follow her throughout the night. Overprotective? Yes, in the best way.

We had a rule that Morgan could not date older boys, in particular any boys who were Kirk's age. Kirk's friends were always hanging around the house, but he was always there to let it be known that his sister was off-limits. Of course, that did not keep the boys from trying!

Mike had always been my protector. Then, my man became my children's protector and the best dad any child could ask for. His love for our children was boundless, from being involved in their daily lives at school plays, ball games, and practices, to being a steady presence in their home and church lives. Kirk and Morgan knew their dad was always present and plugged into their activities as they grew up. They could count on him for advice and wisdom through the years.

Mike wore many hats—husband, dad, provider, comforter, and encourager. He has always been the glue that bonds our family together, and he still juggles all those hats to perfection.

3

LET HER DANCE

Anything is possible with sunshine and a little pink.
—**Lilly Pulitzer**

We knew Morgan was special when she crawled up the side of the couch, stood by herself, and walked at six months and three weeks of age.

It was just a normal day in June, and I was organizing toys when I glanced at Morgan playing on her quilt. "Mike," I called. "I think she's balancing on her own! She let go of the couch and is standing all alone!"

Wringing my hands and wanting to capture this moment, I yelled again to my husband, "Quick! Find the video camera so we can document her first steps. Nobody will believe this!"

Just as soon as I celebrated, reality hit. "It isn't time yet for this to happen. This is too early."

I thought maybe this would be a one-time thing and she would plop down and get interested in her toys, but after a few toddling steps around the room, she was off. No more crawling for Morgan.

My mother was horrified. "It will harm her feet and posture. Don't encourage her to walk so early."

"Encourage her?" I argued. "Morgan did this totally on her own without my prodding. She just took off."

I had taken undergraduate classes in early childhood development, so I knew she was skipping entire growth stages of important milestones. But when I expressed my concerns to her pediatrician, he simply said, "Let her go, Pam. She'll be fine."

And she was, indeed, just fine.

LIKE ANY TYPICAL PRINCESS, Morgan had a style that was all her own. She was our girly-girl, doll-loving child with a big heart. At just a few months of age, she became concerned with her appearance and began systematically handing me hair ribbons when I dressed her. She could not go out without a ribbon in her hair, even when she barely had enough hair to tie back.

That was just the beginning of her obsession with fashion. I had no idea that I was in for a lifetime of finding just the right attire for every occasion. She could pull off any outfit with her signature style. Whether in blue jeans or a formal dress, my daughter possessed a unique style.

Keeping up with Morgan was a full-time job for all of us because she was a daredevil at an early age. There was no amusement park ride she would not tackle, and the bigger the better. The kiddie rides did not interest her for long. The roller coasters and giant Ferris wheel beckoned. With her unabashed sense of wonder, she traveled through life at top speed, always eager for her next adventure.

I was just there trying to put on the brakes.

Kirk's first word was *Dada*, so you can imagine my thrill when Morgan's first word was *Mama*. Still, Morgan was a daddy's girl from day one, and Mike was putty in her hands. He would play with her on hands and knees, being the "horse" she rode through the house.

"Giddyap, Daddy! Go faster," she would shout, pretending she was competing in a living-room rodeo.

Morgan could fix her father's blond hair with ribbons and clips and adorn him with a makeover, and her patient dad would just grin and grin as she continued her magic. Curling up in his lap, she would giggle, "Let's read a book, Daddy," and he would read her favorite book, *No Jumping on the Bed*, over and over.

Morgan was loving and giving to everyone, especially her dad, who would stop whatever he was doing to spend time with her. Mike loved music and dancing, and that love extended to his children. He danced with Morgan from a young age, and she delighted and giggled at being twirled around, swaying with her dad to the rhythm. She wore a knowing smile and knew she was safe in her father's arms. She continued to love music and dance for the rest of her life.

THE BIG FUN BEGAN at age five with the daughter-daddy dances held in our town. That year, Morgan chose the prettiest, baby-blue dress with a lace collar and a satin blue ribbon. She was proud to wear it with her white patent-leather Mary Jane dancing shoes.

Mike left no stone unturned in making her feel special. He appeared in a spiffy sport coat and navy print tie, surprising Morgan with a flower corsage that enhanced her ensemble. She jumped up and down with excitement, and I captured it all on film, grateful I'd married a man who was teaching our daughter how a guy should treat her.

"Daddy, I love the pink roses," Morgan said, as I pinned the corsage to her dress that evening.

"Let's go. We don't want to be late," said Mike. "I want everyone to see my beautiful princess with me tonight."

And off they went for another night of dancing and twirling—mostly hopping up and down for Morgan—until the slow dances would bring her socked feet atop her dad's shoes. This was something all the little girls looked forward to as they admired each other's fancy dresses.

Year after year, Morgan and Mike created happy memories at those father-daughter dances, but we narrowly avoided a catastrophe when Morgan was eight years old. Her dad had to go out of town for a business meeting that year, and she was panicking about the dance. She did not want to miss the big event, but despite his best efforts, Mike couldn't get home in time.

I got a stern look from her when I suggested, "I can take you to the dance."

"Mom," she said, stretching the word into at least three syllables. "Nobody goes with their mom! It's the dad's night."

I understood her sentiments. This wasn't a mother-daughter dance, and it wouldn't be the same without her dad. "Besides, Dad has more fun dancing," she added, laughing.

Like a champ, my father stepped up and offered to take Morgan to the dance.

"Thank you for coming to our rescue," I told him. "She will be so excited to learn Pop will be her date."

Not missing a beat, my dad boasted, "I don't mind taking my favorite princess to the dance. It will be fun for me too!"

Pop was known to be a dandy dresser and always had the perfect wardrobe ready for any occasion. He was the type to keep his Sunday suit on all day after church, just in case some other event required his attendance. And, as a father of three daughters, he was well seasoned in spoiling little girls. This dance would be second nature to him.

As expected, Morgan was thrilled at the thought of her pop, whom she adored, taking over the duties of her father for the night.

Wasting no time, she immediately started planning for the big event. "I think I'll wear my pink dress with the big bright turquoise bow," she said, gathering her accessories. "Maybe I can curl my hair and pull it up in the front with a satin ribbon."

She stood in front of the mirror, pulling her long blond hair up in a sophisticated look. A simple ponytail would not work for a dance night.

"Yes, that's it, and I'll wear my add-a-pearl necklace." She pulled the necklace from her jewelry box, admiring the strand of pearls, which were reserved for special occasions.

On the night of the dance, Pop appeared at our door, smiling. Dressed in his Master's green sports coat and preppy plaid tie and hat, he held a lovely corsage of baby pink roses, a perfect match for Morgan's dress. He wore his black-and-white wingtip leather shoes that he always proudly told everyone he'd worn to his college graduation. And he'd polished them to a shine. His eyes gleamed just as bright when Morgan twirled around, showing off her willowy dress and white leather ballet slippers.

With a twinkle in his eye, Pop proclaimed, "Morgan, you will be the belle of the ball tonight in that beautiful dress."

She beamed as she gave me a goodbye hug and kiss. Pop nodded comfortingly, further assuring me she was in good hands.

With her curls bouncing and her little purse swinging, Morgan skipped to her waiting chariot. As Pop opened the car door and made sure she was buckled inside, he turned and waved to me. "Don't worry. We're going to have a memorable night."

Standing at the door, waving as they drove off, I couldn't stop smiling. The night was shaping up to be a special celebration.

Time for the dance came and went, and they did not come home. I was wearing out the carpet in front of the window, glancing outside again and again, only to see the empty driveway as the clock kept ticking in the kitchen.

My mind was imagining all sorts of crazy things. Then I thought, is this a glimpse of what it will be like during her dating years? Will I be pacing the floor, waiting for her to come home from a date? I was glad that scenario was still years away, but it didn't stop me from worrying about my father and my daughter.

Hoping to learn they'd stopped by my parents' house, I called my mother, but she hadn't heard from them either. "Hang tight," she said. "I'm sure they'll be home soon."

Her positive outlook helped ease my worries, as she assured me that Morgan would be all right.

But the night went on—nine, ten, ten-thirty—and they still did not appear.

I was a knot of nerves by the time the clock struck eleven. Finally, they came bouncing through the door, both smiling as if nothing at all had gone awry.

"Where have you been?" I asked, running to hug Morgan. "I've been so worried."

With his hand on his heart, my dad explained, "After it was over, we went to Rafferty's. We were having so much fun, we just didn't notice the time."

With raised eyebrows, I questioned his choices on a school night. "It's getting late for an eight-year-old, Dad."

Putting his arm around Morgan, he gave me a charming smile. "I know, I know, but this was a special occasion. Can't the rules be extended tonight? It's our first grandfather-granddaughter date."

In a no-win situation, I could only exhale and grin as Morgan beamed and recounted their special night.

"Mom, we danced every dance and didn't sit down once. Pop made it so much fun! Then we went out to eat, and I got my favorite chicken fingers and fries. I told the waitress we were on a date, and I didn't want it to end."

"I'm so glad you both had a good time," I said, grateful to have them both home safely. "Now it's off to bed for you, my little dancing queen. Tell Pop thank you for a wonderful night."

"Thanks, Pop. You're the best!" Then she turned and cartwheeled down the hall to her room.

4

SPOILER ALERT

Stay close to people who feel like sunshine.
—Xan Oku

With four aunts, both Kirk and Morgan were spoiled rotten by their love, attention, and endless generosity. On any given day, my sister Donna, who lived two doors down from us, would sweep them up for an afternoon at the park or an ice cream treat. Donna was also the source of some of Morgan's biggest indulgences. Morgan would not hesitate to call Donna and ask for help hemming a dress or whipping up a costume, usually on only a few hours' notice. She might also ask Donna to French braid her long hair or take her to get some desperately needed chocolate. One Easter, Donna surprised the kids with a baby rabbit—without warning me—but they loved it and were delighted by the gift.

Whenever Mike's sister Denise would come to visit us from Orlando, Florida, she took the kids for rides in her convertible, which thrilled them. She spoiled them with "Aunt Denise outings" and would treat Morgan to girls' days that included lunch dates and trips to Claire's for jewelry, while she'd take Kirk to the movies.

The biggest treat came when Kirk and Morgan each turned eight. To mark the milestone, they each got to fly to Orlando to enjoy their spring break with Aunt Denise. Kirk's adventure included trips to SeaWorld Orlando and going to see the Orlando Magic Basketball team play. Outdoor activities and sports topped his agenda. Morgan's destination was Magic Kingdom, where she took in all the Disney magic she could absorb.

Deborah, Mike's other sister, lived in Jacksonville, Florida. She too sent many thoughtful gifts in the mail, choosing something special for each of the kids on every occasion. She once shipped a teddy bear with pajamas and a sleep hat for Morgan, and she always sent University of Tennessee memorabilia for Kirk.

Deborah said, "Shopping for Morgan is the highlight of my Christmas season. I walk into stores and ask for the wildest thing in stock, and it usually suits Morgan to a tee."

My youngest sister, Kandy, also lived out of town, but she would take the kids swimming and invite Morgan to Nashville for overnight trips. As a graduate of the University of Tennessee, she took both Kirk and Morgan under her wing, showing them the ropes on campus when they decided to attend school there. Kandy even had a pair of vintage orange leather cowboy boots that she'd worn at UT. She gingerly loaned them to Morgan for her tenure there. On any given weekend, Morgan would be seen sporting the striking boots from Aunt Kandy.

It was always a treat when one of the aunts was visiting, always taking Kirk and Morgan on fun adventures.

Kirk spent a weekend with Kandy when she lived in Knoxville. Since he was such a sports fan, Kandy and her husband, Chuck, took him to see a Knoxville Cherokees hockey game, and then stayed for a UT hockey game. The only problem was that UT shared the ice arena, so the game didn't start until midnight. They thought nothing of keeping a seven-year-old boy out that late. Kirk had a great time and couldn't wait to tell me not only about the hockey games but also about staying up way past his bedtime and getting home in the wee hours of the morning. That was the fun of being with an aunt—doing things Mom and Dad wouldn't do with him.

The aunts were a double blessing. They loved like parents and acted like cool friends. They all made Kirk and Morgan feel like sunshine. But the aunts weren't the only ones to spoil our children.

On Morgan's tenth birthday in December 1995, she and I flew to the Mall of America for the day. I splurged on special Delta flights from Memphis to Minneapolis-St. Paul International Airport. I had taken the same trip a few months earlier with a group of teacher friends and my two sisters. It was a fun adventure, but it required a full day, starting with a flight at 6:00 a.m. and returning at 7:00 that night.

Morgan was excited to go because she loved shopping.

"I know just what I want to wear. My new denim vest and skirt," she said, twirling and modeling her outfit for my approval. With a chambray shirt and blue tights, she was ready to travel. Then she held up a denim hat with a yellow daisy on the front. "Mom, I want to wear this too."

"Perfect," I said. "You're ready for a birthday adventure!"

"This'll be fun," she said, jumping into the car with excitement as we drove to the airport early that morning. "No luggage? This is the way to travel!"

As we got closer to Minnesota, we started seeing snow on the ground. Morgan had to take a picture, since we rarely saw snow in our southern city. The mall was convenient to the airport, just across the street, and a shuttle took us straight to the entrance. Thankfully, we didn't have to walk far in the winter weather.

We arrived about seven-thirty and rented lockers for the day. One store, Macy's, opened early, so we shopped there until the other shops opened. Being the largest mall in the US, we stood in awe of its four stories, each decorated in luminous Christmas décor, with a Santa in the first-floor rotunda. Giant ornaments were suspended from the ceiling, and hundreds of trees were scattered in every direction to create a winter wonderland.

"Let's start on the first floor," I told Morgan as we took the escalators down. "We don't want to miss anything."

"Mom, there's a LEGO shop where you can build things. Let's go look."

Every kind of LEGO structure imaginable was displayed as kids crowded around tables, busily creating their own designs. Parents also joined the fun, helping their children build animals, vehicles, buildings, and more. After fighting the crowds for a few minutes, Morgan lost interest. Pulling me along, she said, "I want to see other shops."

Off we went to explore the massive shopping center. Nordstrom drew us in, where a grand piano welcomed each shopper with Christmas music. "This is a fancy store," Morgan marveled, mesmerized by the dazzling decorations in white, gold, and silver.

"Yes, and the marble floors shine so brightly you can see your reflection," I said, admiring the displays.

"I could stay in here all day," Morgan said, each word more energetic than the last.

"With 520 stores to explore, we'd better get going," I said as we walked to the next store. Each floor's route was a one-mile loop, so we would certainly get our exercise exploring all four levels.

I read aloud from the mall's brochure as we decided which store to hit next. "Besides its size of seventy acres, one of its biggest attractions is the indoor theme park."

Morgan beamed. "I want to go on some rides."

"Let's save that for the afternoon. It will be a good break, and we can recuperate from our walking," I suggested.

The highlight of Morgan's day was a visit to the American Girl store. She already had three of their dolls at home with clothes and books, and she loved the background stories that went with each one.

"Wow, Mom, all the American Girl dolls are here. This is so cool."

A display holding all the accessories and clothes was there for all to see. Since we could only look in catalogs in Jackson, Morgan enjoyed seeing this treasure of carriages, beds, horses, and stables in person.

"I already have a canopy bed for Samantha, but she needs a wardrobe for her clothes," she said, admiring the doll-sized furniture.

"That's a good idea for your Christmas list this year," I suggested.

Thrilled at seeing the doll display, we headed to the second floor. By lunchtime, Morgan set her sights on the Rainforest Cafe, where we were welcomed into the jungle restaurant by Cha! Cha! the red-eyed tree frog and Rio the colorful macaw. The animated animals were entertaining as we enjoyed our meal.

Then off we went to explore floors three and four. We bought sparingly, storing smaller purchases in our coat locker before we headed to the amusement park, which featured twenty-seven rides inside the mall.

"I want to ride the roller coaster first," Morgan shouted, jumping up and down.

It proved to be a popular attraction, so we waited in line and were not disappointed with all the dips and turns.

"Now let's ride the Mystery Mine ride. We may even get wet," predicted Morgan.

"I hope not. We don't want wet clothes and feet all day. Let's get a seat at the back," I reasoned.

We got a splash or two on the Log Chute, but we managed to avoid being completely soaked.

With so many rides, there was something for everyone from toddlers to teenagers. "Let's end with a merry-go-round ride," Morgan cheered.

"I'll watch and take your picture," I said. "Pick a good one!"

Watching her ride the carousel, I thought this had been a perfect ending to a busy, fun-filled afternoon at the amusement park. But our girls' day was not over yet. It was only four o'clock, and our shuttle wouldn't pick us up until seven. But, with both of us tired from all the walking, we needed a low-key way to spend those final hours.

"Maybe we can find a good movie," I suggested, and off we went to the cinema on the third floor. We found thirteen film choices, with three appropriate for children: *Jumanji*, *Toy Story*, and *Pocahontas*. Always up for an adventure, Morgan opted for *Jumanji*.

The action-packed story did not disappoint, and we rested as we watched the show. Then we headed to the lockers to retrieve our coats and packages before returning to the airport.

Morgan smiled and sighed. "This has been the best birthday ever, Mom. Thanks so much." Then she gave me a big bear hug.

"It was a whirlwind day," I said, with my heart so full of love. "Now let's head home."

As soon as we got seated on the plane and buckled in, Morgan was sound asleep. "Happy tenth birthday, Morgan," I whispered. "Time to fly this birthday girl home."

Some say it's wrong to spoil a child, but I don't believe that's true. In the end, this beautiful arrangement between aunts, nieces, nephews, and parents has been a gift to everyone involved. We give so much to our children. And in return, our children give us a kind of joy that is pure, unfiltered, and entirely without expectations. They are the blessings we get to spoil, and they spoil us with the simple pleasures of life. It's a deal that we are more than happy to make.

I enjoy spoiling my nieces and nephews too, and Kirk continues to have a special relationship with his adoring aunts. He, in turn, enjoys his young cousins, and the circle continues now that he has become the loving father of two adorable girls.

Can a child receive too much love and attention? I'd say not a chance.

5

THE TREE AND THE VINE

No man truly has joy unless he lives in love.
—St. Thomas Aquinas

As mentioned, Kirk's first word was *Dada*, but his second was *ball*. He loved sports from the time he was a toddler and still does today. Kirk was the carbon copy of his dad, with blond hair, green eyes, and tall for his age. His quiet demeanor disappeared during his games, when he became a competitive player on the field, but as soon as he was out of uniform, the quiet kid returned.

Kandy took him under her wing to teach him how to dunk a basketball when he was seven, using a mini trampoline we had at home. She also taught him to dive off the high dive at our local swimming pool.

Like his aunt, Kirk has continued to love sports throughout his life. T-ball, travel baseball, and basketball and football all kept him busy throughout his youth. He even turned down several opportunities to travel to Europe because he would have had to miss practices for whatever sport was going on at the time. Now he cheers for his daughters in their activities. And, as an avid outdoorsman, he can usually be found camping, hiking, or kayaking in the many rivers and marshes of South Carolina.

KIRK WAS A GREAT big brother and loved his little sister. When he was in kindergarten, I was fortunate to teach at his elementary school. I knew how significant it was for kindergarteners to finally be able to check out a library book on their own. It was a huge deal, making the five-year-olds feel big. The students had to wait until after Christmas break, and they were all excited when the time approached for them to get their very own library book.

"Mom, today's finally the day our class can check out a library book. I've waited since school started," he said, as we drove to school that morning.

"I know you're excited. I can't wait to see what you pick out," I said, admiring the big grin on Kirk's face.

On that cold January day, on the way home from school after Kirk's library day, I asked, "What did you choose for your first book to check out?"

He proudly held up his selection.

Much to my surprise, the book he had chosen was titled *My Ballerina.* Sure enough, the cover featured a little girl in a tutu. My ball-loving son had not picked out a sports book, as I'd expected.

"Why did you choose this book?" I asked.

"Because Morgan will love it," he said, beaming with excitement. "It's all about ballerinas."

He had noticed Morgan's love of ballet because she wore her favorite tutu every day. Usually, it was worn over her regular pants and top, and she did not go anywhere without it. She would have slept in it too, but she admitted it was "too crunchy."

Of course, she jumped for joy at the sight of the book that Kirk had brought home for her. She threw her arms around her big brother, exclaiming, "Thank you, thank you! I love ballerinas sooo much."

And true to her word, she pored over that book and had it read to her again and again. I was so proud that my young son, at the tender age of five, had thought of his sister before himself.

Kirk had sacrificed checking out his first library book at school, all to make his little sister feel special and loved.

~

THAT WAS THE EMOTIONAL landscape of their life together as siblings. They developed a very close relationship and were always looking out for each other. Whether warning her to avoid the speeding "big brown delivery trucks" that came flying through our neighborhood while she was riding her bike, or running interference with older boys who wanted to talk to her as she reached her teen years, Kirk was always Morgan's shield and defender. He took great pride in that role, and Morgan thrived under his loyal protection. She was free to explore, be loud, and be herself, knowing her beloved big brother was always watching over her.

I have countless memories of their special sibling bond, but a few surface now as I write. One day, the scent of damp earth filled the air after a late-summer shower soaked our forested backyard. Morgan, at age three, with bright eyes and boundless energy, was ready to go out and play. She had always been curious about outdoor things like butterflies, frogs, or anthills. Kirk, by contrast, was more cautious, a quiet observer. Yet when Morgan's curiosity led her to investigate a moving object in the backyard, his caution evaporated, replaced by an instinctive surge of protection. He didn't think; he just acted.

That day, she'd just reached the edge of the woods when he pulled her back, gripping her arm tightly. Morgan was annoyed, even a little angry, until she saw what Kirk had seen. A deadly cottonmouth snake lay curled on a log, hissing at them.

In a panic, Kirk grabbed her up as she screamed in fear. They ran to meet me on the deck. His instinct to protect his sister had kicked in, and he responded quickly, never considering his own safety.

Holding tight to her brother, Morgan was just as out of breath as he was when they reached me. I was thankful they were safe, and I felt proud that Kirk had acted responsibly and bravely at the age of six. In that moment, he realized his role wasn't just to be her brother, but also her protector.

In return, Morgan was her brother's biggest supporter. At every T-ball, Little League, soccer, travel ball, basketball, and football game, she sat in the stands cheering him on. At the Little League championship game, Morgan proudly sported the words "Kirk's Sister" on a team shirt.

As they grew older, the threats changed, but the dynamic stayed the same. When Morgan faced heartbreak, Kirk was there with a sympathetic, listening ear. As she navigated the complexities of school and college, he was her sounding board, always on her side. Kirk never resented his role. It was simply who he was.

Kirk was Morgan's protector all her life. Like a sturdy oak tree, his roots stretched deep into the earth, unyielding and strong. He stood tall, his branches wide and protective, always keeping a watchful eye over his free-spirited little sister.

Morgan, on the other hand, was like a vibrant vine, her tendrils constantly reaching, exploring, and embracing everything around her. She was a whirlwind of joyous energy, untamed and fearless. Kirk was her unwavering anchor, his presence a comforting constant in her adventurous life. Morgan learned to appreciate her brother's steady strength, knowing he would always be there, standing tall and watching over her.

Big brother was always there for her, until the very end.

THE DAY WE LOST MORGAN, my Aunt Peggy called my cousin Jay to tell him the devastating news. He answered as he and his wife were on the way to the hospital for the birth of their third girl. They had already decided to name her Hannah Kathryn Austin, but after listening to his mother relay the horrible news, he proclaimed, "We have to use Morgan in her name."

Because of that loving gesture, Hannah Kathryn Morgan Austin was born on the day we lost our Morgan. What a precious tribute to our daughter, a kind act that honors the circle of life—a sweet baby born on the same day another life was taken.

Hannah became our goddaughter, and she has grown into a truly special and remarkable young lady. The family lives in a nearby state, and we have enjoyed watching her grow up. Not long ago, she shared something priceless with me: a photo of her dressing room at home. On the side of the mirror, she'd placed Morgan's picture. She told me she sees it and thinks of her every day. Morgan would have genuinely loved Hannah's inner beauty and spirit, which shines through in her radiant smile.

Years later, when Kirk was expecting his first child, he shared that his firstborn daughter would have the name Morgan as well. After shedding buckets of happy tears, Mike and I were thrilled to have another Morgan in the family.

Funny, as she grows, I see her dad, Kirk, in her looks, but she also carries traits of Morgan. I see Morgan's determination in every task she undertakes, her love for music and dance of all kinds, and her genuine ability to meet and accept new friends easily.

Kirk has made sure that both of his girls are getting acquainted with their aunt through stories and pictures from their childhood. After years of protecting and adoring his little sister, Kirk was born to be a girl dad. Morgan loved her big brother, and she would also have loved and adored his children. I hope she is watching over Kirk's family, sharing in the joy of every scenic bike ride, invigorating hike, plunge in the ocean, and dance recital, and celebrating all their successes in life.

Kirk, the sturdy oak tree, and Morgan, the vibrant vine—a perfect combination.

God is my protection.
He makes my way free from fault.
He makes me like a deer that does not stumble;
he helps me stand on the steep mountains.
—Psalm 18:32–33

6

DRESS UP

If I could lick the sunset,
I'll bet it would taste like Neapolitan ice cream.
—Jarod Kintz

From childhood make-believe to lifelong self-expression, Morgan's love of dress-up remained a constant thread woven throughout the tapestry of her life. Our sweet neighbor, Mrs. Redding, was the grandmother of one of Morgan's best friends Anna. The girls spent hours at the Redding home, playing dress-up in high-heeled shoes and frilly dresses. Armed with mismatched scarves and bedazzled hats, Morgan and Anna constructed elaborate costumes, weaving stories and adventures around them for hours.

One day, the girls would be graceful ballerinas. The next time, they'd become mommies taking care of their baby dolls; the next, mermaids or teachers, lining their dolls in a circle while they sat at the front and read books aloud. But Morgan's favorite item was the costume jewelry section of Mrs. Redding's tall chest.

"There's a box with fancy earrings, Mom," she said with wide eyes one day after discovering the secret treasure chest. "And necklaces made of diamonds."

A pirate's bounty tumbled out as the girls opened the drawer to discover loot filled with precious "jewels." Each piece complemented their vibrant outfits, adding to the celebration of the characters they were portraying. With easy clip-on earrings and shimmering jewels around their necks and wrists, the five-year-old girls were ready for the red carpet.

Morgan would say to Anna, "Look, I'm Cinderella." Then she would waltz through the house as if entering a night of enchantment.

Shrill laughs and giggles filled the air as the girls played dress-up for hours on end. What a delightful fantasy they created, wearing "diamonds" that sparkled in the sunlight. At home, Morgan's jewelry was the plastic kind made for children, but next door she could enjoy the brilliance of "real diamonds."

Morgan and Anna played for days, turning their imaginations into dazzling affairs by wearing long white gloves. Then one day, Mrs. Redding decided to clean out her closet. "Girls, I'm thinking of clearing out some of my things, and I thought you both would like some of the shoes and clothes. But that's not all. I'm also giving away some of my jewelry. Take any pieces you would like. I haven't worn some of these in years. I just don't dress up like I used to, and I know you girls love to play with my rhinestones."

The girls couldn't believe their good fortune. They held hands and jumped up and down. Morgan's jackpot was a glittering purse overflowing with empowerment for a five-year-old girl. To her, the sparkling rhinestones weren't just decorations; they were trophies, each piece an addition to an already growing dress-up closet.

Racing into the house with her arms full, Morgan cheered as she showed me her new assets. "These are real diamonds, Mom!"

With a wide smile, I said, "Yes, these are wonderful for dressing up. Let's remember they are for playtime. They are too special to wear outside of the house."

Morgan nodded in agreement as she skipped to her bedroom and put away her stash of new riches for safekeeping.

This happened over the weekend. When Sunday came, she wanted to wear her new jewelry to church to show her friends. "Remember," I said, "these are for play. We shouldn't wear them to church or school."

Disappointed, Morgan returned the jewelry to her box and continued to dress for church.

That evening, we laid out her clothes on Sunday evening so she could dress herself for school on Monday. The next morning, as we rushed through a breakfast of oatmeal and blueberries, we gathered our backpacks and scurried out the door.

Soon, we parked the car on campus, and I sent Kirk off to his second-grade classroom while Morgan headed the other direction to her kindergarten class. Dressed in pink gingham pants and a matching lacy top, with a pink bow nestled in her blond hair, she was ready to see her friends and the teacher she loved. I went on to my third-grade classroom in another part of the building.

The day was uneventful until I got a message from Morgan's teacher. "Come down to my room when you get a chance today. I need to show you something."

It was close to lunchtime, so I made my way to her classroom. I glanced through the door's window to see Morgan sitting in her small wooden chair. She was in all her glory, like the Queen of England on Coronation Day. She was at her desk, writing her alphabet letters without a care in the world. However, she was wearing dangling rhinestone earrings dripping down almost to her shoulders, a dazzling diamond necklace, and a sparkling tiara to top off the outfit!

Mrs. Deloach came out into the hall, smiling at the spectacle before me. "Morgan came into the room this morning, retrieved her 'fine jewelry' from her backpack, and proceeded to put it on right away, before the national anthem and announcements," she explained. "Her friends were oohing and aahing over her finery, and Morgan was owning it with pride. Then everybody got to work, and that was that."

The teacher offered a kind laugh, clearly entertained by Morgan's antics. "I knew you hadn't sent her to school dressed that way," she continued. "But she carried on just like it was the most normal thing to do. No harm done, and I enjoyed her acting like it was the most typical thing to wear on a Monday morning in kindergarten."

When I reclaimed Morgan's bounty of precious jewels, my daughter said in a timid voice, "I just wanted my friends to see my new jewelry. Nobody else in kindergarten has any like them."

Each jewel was a brushstroke on the canvas of Morgan's unique personality.

As a close family friend and one of Morgan's high school teachers would tell me after my daughter's death, "Morgan was her own person, comfortable with who she was and never satisfied with the mediocre. She took every day as it came at her, and then she proceeded to live it to the max."

Yes, her life's flame burned with its own unique glow. Dressing up was just one reflection of Morgan's bright personality as she created her own bold style in life. From toddlerhood to adulthood, her fashion made a statement—a distinctive flair all her own.

TODAY, IT SEEMS EASY to find influencers for anything from clothes, cars, and vacations to restaurants, events, and makeup. But there was no such thing as a "social media influencer" in 1999 when Morgan was fourteen.

I realized she was an influencer ahead of her time during our Thirty-Hour Famine at church. The youth director had challenged students to bring their friends to join our already large assembly of more than one hundred local teens. The event was a weekend fundraiser for World Vision, a Christian humanitarian organization that helps feed and care for families in Sudan, Kenya, and other countries in need.

Morgan spoke to a few friends, and then they talked to other friends, and soon she had created so much buzz that the church youth event became "the place to be" that weekend.

When my friend Mona saw more than twenty teenagers accompanying Morgan, she said, "I'm astonished that middle schoolers would want to spend their weekend at church, not eating anything for thirty hours and paying a fee of thirty dollars to do charity work!"

The fact that Morgan could inspire them so easily did not surprise me at all. She had become a charismatic leader who always wanted her friends around her. Another time, she was playing on her middle school's softball team, and she told the girls after practice one day that they had to coordinate uniforms. That meant they would all wear the same red grosgrain ribbons in their hair, so they would match.

After the next ball game, a delighted player's mother thanked me. "My daughter hasn't worn a ribbon in her hair in at least ten years, and she especially would not have been caught wearing one in middle school. But when Morgan said to get one for the team uniform, off we went to the fabric store, no questions asked."

Morgan was a natural leader, with so many kids wanting to be in her company, whether in church, at school, or on the field. Because she cared so genuinely for others, her friends listened to her, trusted her, and eagerly followed her lead. Too bad influencers were not a thing back then. Morgan's college tuition could have been fully funded!

Brothers and sisters, think about the things that are good and worthy of praise. Think about the things that are true and honorable and right and pure and beautiful and respected.
—Philippians 4:8

7

TOURIST ESCAPADES

If you want to see the sunshine, you have to weather the storm.
—Frank Lane

As a teacher of gifted students in the Jackson-Madison County school system, I was fortunate to take high school and college students on several trips to Europe in the 1980s and 1990s. I could not convince Kirk to go with us because he would've had to miss summer football practice, and at that time, he was not really interested in travel. That gave Morgan the opportunity to join us on several trips.

The first trip she took with us proved memorable in a big way. Shortly before our departure date, Morgan injured her lower leg while playing at church. As Morgan related the story to me, she said, "The sixth-grade boys were chasing the sixth-grade girls in Sunday school, and the girls slammed the door, and the glass broke."

Someone ran to get me, and I could see lots of blood. She was not able to stand, so Mike and I took her to the emergency room for X-rays and the news that she had a three-quarter tear in her Achilles tendon.

"You're lucky," the doctor said. "It wasn't cut all the way through, but surgery will be required to stitch the tendon back together."

After surgery, she had to wear a cast on her leg and use crutches for eight weeks. Then she graduated to a walking cast for the remaining four weeks.

In the emergency room, the doctor asked, "How did this happen?"

I relayed the story of how the boys had been chasing the girls at church. He looked at me, puzzled that such a ruckus would go on at church.

"What church is that?" he asked.

"Oh," I responded with a little white lie. "First Baptist."

I was embarrassed that these shenanigans had happened at our church, First Methodist. As soon as I fibbed, Morgan and I looked at each other and broke into big grins while the doctor never knew the difference.

SOON, IT WAS TIME for our ten-day European adventure. Morgan had gotten a walking cast on her leg five days before we were scheduled to leave. Even though it was a little heavy and cumbersome, it gave her enough mobility to walk without crutches.

I was concerned she would have trouble with all the walking required in Europe, but Morgan was determined not to be held back from this opportunity. "I'll be able to walk a lot more easily with this cast," she reasoned, pointing to the bright green cast covered with her friends' signatures. "I assure you, I can keep up. I don't want to miss this."

"Well, you are young," I said, giving it careful thought. "I know I couldn't travel with that on my foot, but maybe youth is on your side."

I was leading the group, so I needed to go, with or without her. Morgan knew this too, so she pressed on. "Mom, you've already paid for the trip in full." She kept insisting she was feeling fine. "See? I can walk without any trouble. I don't need the crutches," she boasted, as she pranced around her bedroom, modeling one of her favorite flowery dresses she planned to pack for the trip.

Wrinkling my brow, I said, "Are you sure you can keep up with the group? It's a long trip, and you haven't had much practice with your cast."

Crossing her arms, Morgan pleaded with pitiful puppy eyes. "There will be so many exciting places to see, I won't even notice my foot. I can rest at the hotels each night when we stop. Even the doctor said it would be safe to go…if I take it easy."

"That's what I'm worried about, Morgan. You don't know how to take it easy."

Arguing her point into the ground, she continued, "Mom, I can't possibly miss the trip of a lifetime. I can wear dresses and shorts that won't be hard to put on with this cast." She beamed as she swished her long ponytail. "I'm ready! I promise."

"Okay, okay." I threw my arms up in surrender. "I see you're determined, but you have to promise me you won't overdo it."

So, with a walking cast on her foot, off we went on our grand travel adventure.

Unfortunately, we quickly learned that the five countries we were exploring did not have any handicap provisions at the sites we were visiting. No ramps. No wheelchairs. Only stairs. And certainly no easily accessible restrooms. Elevators were scarce, and we ended up missing a few key attractions while the group went ahead without us. Morgan and I had to view the stately Arc de Triomphe in Paris from below instead of taking in the sweeping view from the top.

In Rome, we admired the grand staircase from the bottom instead of tackling the challenging climb of the 135 Spanish Steps rising over three terraces. Poor Morgan had to drag her cast along while everyone else walked normally. Still, while her injury may have slowed her pace, it never dampened her spirits as we strolled through beautiful plazas and along cobblestone streets.

Her favorite city, Florence, was the hardest to navigate because no cars were allowed in the interior of the city. With so many beautiful places to explore, we were in for a lot of walking. Leather markets filled the center of Florence, and the stalls were packed with handcrafted purses, luggage, coats, and jackets.

Before we'd left for our trip, I had told Morgan we'd be going to the markets. "We won't be buying any leather coats for you to grow out of at this age," I'd warned. She was disappointed by my decision until she saw the prices of the smaller leather jackets in Florence.

"Mom," she exclaimed with her eyes shining bright, "this jacket fits me perfectly, and it's not that expensive." The plaster-wrapped cast certainly didn't stop her from twirling around the market to show off her new fashion find.

Sure enough, the prices were so much more affordable than I ever dreamed, more like Walmart prices than the prices of real handcrafted leather we could find at home.

"Well," I confessed, examining the brown, zippered jacket and admiring its high quality, "these are very reasonable prices, especially for handmade leather that feels like butter. We'll just have to indulge."

A fantastic leather market and Michelangelo's David, all in one city. What's not to love about Florence?

"Oh, Mom!" she cheered, throwing her arms around me in gratitude. "You're wonderful. I'll keep this jacket forever." That was another thing to love about Morgan. No matter what we did for her—big or small—she always expressed sincere appreciation.

About the fifth day of our rigorous agenda, we took a busy city tour and then boarded a train for the next country. By then, the boot had begun to rub against her throbbing leg, and Morgan was complaining of pain for the first time since the surgery. Concerned, I called the doctor back home, and he instructed, "If rest is not an option, and she can't come home, then get a set of crutches to help relieve the ankle stress on her ankle. That should help ease the pain. And be sure to keep her feet up when possible."

With our hectic schedule, keeping her feet elevated would be hard to do, so crutches were the answer.

We had reached London by this time, and, as directed by the hotel's concierge, I called a chemist, which is what they call a pharmacist in much of Europe. Through the pharmacy, I ordered a pair of crutches and had them sent to the hotel by taxi. They were very expensive crutches—far pricier than the leather jacket.

Soon, I retrieved them from the hotel lobby and brought them to Morgan. She took one look, crossed her arms, and announced in her middle-school tone, "No, Mom. I won't use them."

Unlike our crutches in the States that have cushioned pads under a person's arms for support, these had metal cuffs that attached to the forearms. Morgan simply refused to use them.

After some encouragement, she finally agreed to give them a try. But they proved difficult to use, and she struggled to coordinate both arms and hands. The forearm crutch seemed to overwhelm her as she walked clumsily around the hotel room. Her frustration grew as she failed several times to stand up. She could not adjust to the cuffs on her arms, and she finally unstrapped them and announced, "I can't do this," as she fell onto the bed. The crutches spilled onto the hotel floor.

As I picked up the crutches for her to try again, I offered gentle encouragement. "Don't give up, Morgan. It'll take practice, but this should relieve the pressure on your ankle. It won't be so bad when you get used to them."

After practicing over and over with no success, Morgan threw up her hands again and wailed, "I'll go without them."

I ended up dragging those crutches all over Europe, throwing them into the overhead compartment of every bus or train as we traveled from country to country. Not only did I have my luggage to struggle with, but I had to help Morgan with hers, plus I had a pair of long appendages stuck under my arms at each stop.

This was not fun.

Any time Morgan complained, all I had to do was point to the crutches nestled in the overhead compartment of the bus or train we were riding, and she suddenly felt better. Yes, stubbornness runs both ways in this family.

The next country, Switzerland, was a little easier because walking was kept to a minimum. The picturesque Swiss town had winding cobblestone streets and snowy Alpine peaks towering over the spires of quaint white churches. We were stunned by the icy, glacier-fed lake and the graceful swans gliding across the turquoise water.

Morgan, with her long blond braided pigtails, blended in perfectly in the peaceful, Heidi-like setting. We ate Swiss chocolate, which was exquisite, and pungent Swiss cheese fondue, which was not so special, and we thoroughly enjoyed the countryside and all it had to offer.

Yes, Switzerland was a breath of fresh air, a respite from the hustle of other European cities. Our transportation included funiculars, gondola rides, cable cars, and the world's steepest cogwheel train as we traversed the panoramic mountains. Then we cruised across tranquil Lake Lucerne. This saved Morgan's leg from the tiring walks we had experienced in other countries.

On the last "leg" of our journey, as we were leaving the train in Switzerland, I let the crutches remain onboard and smiled as they rode off toward cities and countries unknown. Both of us were glad to release the burden of hauling them with us. We arranged for some padding to be placed on Morgan's boot, and she had no complaints for the remainder of the trip.

The doctor was correct in telling us that a set of crutches would help her recovery. As it turned out, they worked like a charm in a most unexpected manner.

When we got home, Morgan put her arms around me in a cajoling way. "Mom, I didn't get the full value of that Europe trip because of my walking cast, so I may just have to go back."

I agreed.

And we did return four years later.

For our next European trip, Morgan was a junior in high school. She jumped with both feet at the chance to go to Europe again.

"Mom, this will be an epic trip because I won't have that heavy boot or crutches. No limping!"

And I had to agree. "Nothing will hold us back this time."

On Thursday, April 30, 2002, we rushed through Atlanta's busy airport with our group of twenty-five, careful to be on time for our Alitalia flight. But when we reached the gate, no one was there. Was anybody else going to Rome?

We inquired, and the nearby airport workers said, "Someone will be here before you take off." They didn't seem concerned at all.

We learned that not only was Italy a laid-back country, but so was its airline. No one seemed to be in any hurry until the last minute, when we quickly boarded the plane for the nine-and-a-half-hour flight.

Midway through the flight, small bottles of wine were passed out to the passengers—adults only—and everyone was pleased with the warm hospitality. But we were all surprised when the empty bottles were not collected, and many of them ended up on the floor, where Italian newspapers also littered the aisle. We had to kick our way to the bathroom during the flight. Subsequent bottles of wine were passed out, and soon nobody cared how the plane looked. Not much sleep took place on that flight, but everyone had a good time, and that was what the airline wanted—a happy plane full of tipsy tourists, all excited to start our Roman holiday.

A little tired, we landed and started touring right away, not that we minded seeing the sights. The Roman Forum was first, then the Colosseum. Tourists could have their picture taken with a Roman gladiator, complete with sword, so of course, all the girls surrounded the handsome Italian. He gladly took our euros in exchange for an authentic Roman picture.

~

Excerpts From Morgan's Journal

April 30, 2002

> Still sleepy from the plane ride, we got on the bus to see the city. It was an awesome tour of the Colosseum. It's so big, and the guide told us that they used to flood the floor and have ships battling inside the arena for entertainment. I can't imagine that!!
>
> The steps were so high between levels, it made it hard to climb up to the top, but what a view from the top! I missed this view from my last trip. No boot cast on this trip!!!
>
> Then we went to find "the best gelato in Rome." I got 2 scoops of chocolate and a chocolate cone. On the way through the streets, Jodi and I spotted 80 good dress shops. Hope we can come back and shop tomorrow.
>
> There is no drinking age limit here. It's cool that wine bottles are on the tables with our pizza dinner, just like it's water. Of

course, Mom is not letting me drink, but I think some of the senior students are with their parents' permission.

May 1, 2002

After touring this morning, we went to the Piazza Navona. The Pantheon was in the same plaza, and we had pasta for dinner at a cool restaurant. We sat outside and had gelato again and listened to a little street band. We laughed because they played Pink Floyd. It was hilarious.

As we were sitting, two Italian guys in the Italian Marines came up to me to talk. We could not understand each other, but we tried. They left and then brought back a red rose. It was so sweet.

I haven't bought anything yet. I'm planning on getting some cool things in Florence.

We ended the night at Trevi Fountain. I threw coins over my left shoulder with my right hand like every tourist there, in hopes of returning to this city again.

After our second day in Rome, our group returned to our hotel before another afternoon tour. We had just arrived when a girl ran into the lobby and yelled, "The Pope is outside!"

Not fully believing her, we ran outside, expecting to be duped. Instead, we saw a Roman Catholic procession moving down the street. The Pope was not in his "popemobile," as I would have expected. Instead, he was sitting in the back of a white pickup truck! He was dressed all in white, waving to the excited crowd as he passed by. Throngs of people lined the streets and cheered as he drove through Rome.

We later discovered that May 1 was a major Catholic holiday. The Feast of Saint Joseph the Worker is a day to honor the patron saint of workers. We were in exactly the right place to see the Pope, and we were thrilled when the parade passed right by our hotel, a bonus few people ever get to experience, even in Rome.

Throughout our time in Rome, we met other student tour groups from the States. Some we saw often, and we got to know one group from Georgia. One boy, Christopher, was a handsome honey-blond senior with piercing blue eyes. He always seemed to be hanging around the sites we were touring each day. Despite the many beautiful buildings to see, he usually kept his focus on Morgan, flirting with her throughout the trip.

On the day we visited the Vatican, we were amazed by the enormous square in front of St. Peter's Basilica. The entrance to the basilica's elliptical center encloses visitors within the "maternal arms of the Mother Church" (in the designer Bernini's own words). We learned that the Pope addresses the people each Sunday, sometimes welcoming more than 80,000 faithful worshippers with crowds nearly triple that size during special events.

It was an impressive site, but the most dazzling were the Renaissance masterpieces and Michelangelo's frescoes in the Sistine Chapel. Built in 1473, it took the artist four years to paint the ceiling, where he meticulously depicted scenes from the book of Genesis.

We also learned that twenty-five years later, the Pope commissioned Michelangelo to paint the splendid fresco, *The Last Judgment,* behind the altar, which took him five years to complete.

In the more than 500 years since his original work, the exquisite frescoes had been painstakingly restored to their vibrant colors. It took the restorers fourteen years to renovate the rectangular brick building with its six arched windows and barrel-vaulted ceiling.

We were euphoric, as we stood in complete awe, craning our necks upward to view the paintings. "Look at the deep, vivid hues," I said as I took in the bright blue, stunning shades of orange, and explosions of yellow and green. "Breathtaking!"

The designs were so complex that it would have taken hours upon hours to study the details in each panel. "I can't believe one person had to lie on his back to create these scenes. He made the ceiling come alive," Morgan exclaimed. "I'm almost speechless. The clouds look like they are floating on the ceiling."

We were enveloped in deep reverence as the crowd inched around the immense room.

"I'm soaking this in, Mom," Morgan said, as we gazed upward. "I don't want to forget this."

As we toured the Sistine Chapel, the silence was broken when we ran into the same group of students from Georgia. And you guessed it: we saw Christopher again.

Afterward, Morgan told me what happened. She said that he had run to catch up with our group and gushed, "Morgan, I can't believe our paths crossed again. It's fate!"

"I know," Morgan said, giving him a demure smile. "We're following each other's exact itinerary."

Christopher looked up at the dazzling ceiling as he grabbed her hand. With a dimpled grin, he stared into her eyes and said, "Morgan, here I am gazing at the most beautiful artwork in the world by Michelangelo, and all I can see is you."

"Aw, that's so sweet, Christopher," Morgan gushed. "You make me feel so special."

A little embarrassed by his flirting, Morgan sidled up to me and told me what he had said.

I blurted, "That's the most romantic line I've ever heard! Write it in your travel journal, so you don't forget."

We both laughed, and she became friends with Christopher, staying in touch on and off for the rest of that summer. When he went to college that fall, they lost track of each other. But she never forgot the greatest line of all time, delivered in the Sistine Chapel by the boy with the piercing blue eyes.

Excerpts from Morgan's Journal

The Georgia group keeps showing up in each city we are in each day. We saw them in Pisa and again in Florence. We had fun in Florence when our group went to a dance club called "Space Electric." It was just for teens, and a lot of groups from the States were there. It was so much fun! I taught Robyn, Rachael, and all of my group my dances. Even though the music was Techno, it was a fun night.

I think Switzerland is one of my favorite countries we visited. The water from the snow-filled mountains is beautiful. I would love to go snow skiing in the winter. The chocolate is amazing too. We bought Pop, my grandfather, chocolate cigars. He will love them. We got small Swiss Army knives for family at home. Mine is pink. Tomorrow to Berne, Switzerland, to see the bears, and then the bullet train to Paris.

We made it to London. A lot of excitement. A celebration for Queen Elizabeth's Golden Jubilee is this week. It marks 50 years of being on the throne. We saw the parade with the Queen's horses and guards. Lots of things to buy with the queen's picture. Mom got a small plate marking the Jubilee. We did not see the queen, but we did go to Windsor Castle and saw her flag flying. It meant she was at the castle that day. Wished we could have seen her. We did see the dollhouse that all the royal children played with inside the castle. Too cool.

On our last day in London, we wanted an American hamburger and any drink with ice, which we had not had on our trip. We went straight to the Hard Rock Cafe. I know all about Hard Rock because the founder, Issac Tigrett, is from our hometown. The second one in the world was in Jackson at our mall. Mom says it stayed open for a short time and closed after a few years. We were eager to see the London restaurant, and on the wall was a Jackson, Tennessee, sign. We were so excited! The menu also had at the bottom God bless Big D (Dallas), The Big Apple, and Jackson, Tennessee. We took pictures, and now I wish we had gotten a menu to take home, but I did get a T-shirt.

~

As we were boarding our flight home, I remarked, "Morgan, I think we more than made up for your last trip to Europe. You managed to see all the things you had to skip the first time, with a lot of surprises thrown in."

"I had the best time," Morgan said, thanking me as she slid into her seat on the plane. "I'll remember this trip forever."

"What city did you enjoy the most?" I asked with curiosity.

"Without a doubt, Florence," she said without missing a beat. "Mom, I even think I would like to spend a semester there when I go to college."

"That's a great idea," I said. "Let's work on that when you apply to schools."

Morgan was scheduled to attend the spring semester in Florence, studying Italian art during her junior year of college.

But fate intervened again, and she never made it.

8

THE SHOCK

Love comforteth like sunshine after rain.
—William Shakespeare

Morgan continued to make numerous friends like Christopher throughout her life. These friends showed up in volumes after the accident. The hospital halls were full of college students desperate to say their final goodbyes. As I looked out of her ICU room, I saw students with their arms around each other, crying. Some sat on the hallway floor, and some lay there sobbing, while others tried to console them. They spilled into other hallways too. By that point, this procession of people had been waiting for hours just to see her. I knew our daughter had influenced many lives in her short twenty years, but it was never so evident as it was in those harrowing hours. Mike and I were both moved deeply, witnessing the hundreds of students crowding the hospital halls, waiting their turn to see Morgan.

The accident happened on homecoming weekend, and the football game that Saturday was happening two miles away from the hospital. Morgan was supposed to have been at the game with her friends, celebrating and having a good time with the 104,818 fans in the stadium.

But her friends were not at the football game. They were here, in the cold, solemn hospital halls, waiting.

With us.

With her.

Trying to comfort Morgan's grieving friends was too hard for my family members. My two sisters, husband, and son could not verbalize. Instead, they crumbled and huddled in the corner of the room. Through blinding tears, I recognized their agony, and I knew they could not talk to anyone.

But I also knew those students needed comfort too.

I closed the hospital door and said a short prayer. "Lord, give me strength to face Morgan's friends and show my love to each one of them."

Alone at the door, I braced myself. Then I stretched out my arms, embraced each one of Morgan's friends, and told them the truth: "You were important to her."

My eyes were swimming and burning, as if I were underwater. In that moment, I was drowning.

The previous evening, I had talked to Morgan while she was out celebrating homecoming weekend. She was so happy and excited to be on a date and to share the special evening with friends.

Now, my body was numb; my thoughts, tangled. But I kept offering hugs and words of encouragement as the nurses let her friends in a few at a time. *How can this be happening?* They all expressed sorrow and shared stories of their times with Morgan.

Many related the last conversation they'd had with her, whether it had taken place the night before or weeks earlier.

"I saw her last night, and she was happy and visiting with everyone and having a wonderful time," her roommate Megan told us. "We had plans for her to come home, and we were going to order pizza. But she never came."

I immediately hugged this young girl and joined her in tears of disbelief. If only she could have known how much I wanted to hear those words—to know for certain that Morgan's last few hours had been happily spent with friends.

As the nurses kept escorting a few at a time into our hospital room, the phrase I heard over and over was, "Morgan was my best friend," and many shared stories that touched me about their relationships with her.

"She supported me when I had a bad time in my life. She didn't criticize me; she just listened to me and loved me. I'll never forget that about her," Kim said through tears.

Her friend Elizabeth shared stories of the fun they always had at school. "Morgan always had an adventurous spirit. She lifted others up, and I loved being with her."

I held Elizabeth close for a time, just trying to let the moment sink in.

Another friend, Carrie, cried as she told me, "Morgan cared about her friends in a genuine way. She was steadfast and loyal. I never had to worry about her not caring about me. She was always there with a comforting smile, encouraging words, or just a hug. I will never forget her smile."

As each friend filed into the room, another wave of raw sadness washed over me. Her life was rich with friends, and she cared about all of them in a heartfelt way.

Still another struggled to tell me her story, her eyes glistening with tears. "She was a girl's girl, a faithful and loyal best friend. Morgan listened to my problems and never passed judgment on me. She always had my back. I could count on her to stand by me. She was my cheerleader in life."

Wow! Cheerleader in life. She was mine too.

The big college boys would come in just as broken as the girls, crying, with their heads in their hands, as they spoke of their shock. Many had stories, but most just wanted to see her. It was hard not to imagine her waking up and talking to us. Many of the guys—boyfriends, or just close friends—would say, "I always loved her."

I would agree, which seemed to comfort them in a mothering way as I wrapped my arms around them.

I hurt, just as they were hurting. But I, her mother, couldn't fix this.

Again and again, each student revealed precious stories, as I hugged and embraced tear-stained faces. Each conversation was so intimate to me. They were pouring out their hearts and love, and it was somehow filling me up.

My heart burned with gratitude for these unfolding memories they laid at my feet.

You see, it was essential for them to have a final goodbye.

All this time, Morgan was lying in bed as if she were asleep. Not a scratch could be seen on her. She looked like a peaceful angel, sleeping with her hair perfectly spread across her pillow. All of Morgan's injuries were internal, which made it even harder to imagine her so close to leaving all of us.

Morgan had a saying: "Boys will come and go, but girlfriends will always be there for you." She was a true friend and loyal to all.

Fighting back tears, I listened as each of her friends filed in and stood by her bed. That was when I felt as though I were having an out-of-body experience. I was like a bird perched on a branch, watching the action below. A gushing raw layer of sadness came over me every time.

Many ex-boyfriends claimed they would be back together, dating again soon, and I agreed with them all. Through their flowing tears, I could see their sincere desperation and loss.

I looked at Morgan in this aseptic hospital environment—the harsh lights turned down, the bed with monitors attached, the sterile smell of the room. I longed to take her away to a familiar setting, to the comfort of home. I wanted to bring her back to her bed, her room, with her favorite things surrounding her.

I did not want to say goodbye. Especially not here.

This was not right.

This couldn't be happening.

Yes, my pain and grief tormented me, but that day I began to understand that many were suffering this loss with us.

Maybe she'll wake up and talk to us. Maybe this really is all a nightmare.

Earlier in the night, the nurses had removed a tiny square piece of hair so an electrode could be placed into her head for monitoring.

They took her hair. Her beautiful hair.

The one thing she was so particular about.

Her long, flowing, blond hair.

She was always so careful about the way she wore it, only cutting a few inches at a time, because it was too precious to cut much. She wanted to keep its perfect coloring, a bright summer blond, all year long.

Her hair.

Whatever way she wore it—with braids, ribbons, headbands, a ponytail, or tucked up under a baseball cap or cowboy hat, wet or dry—it always looked perfectly coiffed.

Her hair.

She did not let anyone disturb her hair except her hairdresser.

A small smile broke out on my face as Kandy said, "She would be hysterical if she woke up and found they had disturbed her hair, especially by shaving a small section! That electrode would come flying out, and I would be fearful for the nurses who did this to her hair."

"She would throw an absolute hissy fit if she knew someone had messed with her hair," Donna said. "I would hate to witness that."

Everyone in the room agreed. That was the only time in that tension-filled day that a slight smile appeared on anyone's face.

I DON'T KNOW HOW I managed to receive the hundreds of people who came to Morgan's hospital bed. I could have easily refused visitors, retreating to a quiet corner and surrounding myself with my closest family in our darkest hours. Only after the halls had cleared and students and friends had gone back to their dorms and apartments did I realize that God had given me an inner strength when I needed it most. Without God, I certainly would not have been capable of having a conversation with anyone without breaking into great sobs of sorrow. But he carried me during those tense hours, and it gave me an inner peace to receive her friends. Their stories and love for Morgan became a crucial part of my healing process, a gift I've looked back on again and again with a grateful heart.

With doctors and nurses continuing to come in and out of her room, we were told that Morgan's vital signs were getting worse. We knew we had very little time left with her on this earth.

Reality began to sink in. This was really going to happen. I was going to lose my daughter in the prime of her life.

I sat on her bed and stroked her long hair, arranging it just so, in a way that would have pleased her, and cradled her still, motionless face, thinking it would soothe her, but I was met with no reaction. I lay down beside Morgan, just so I could be near her and feel her shallow breathing.

I poured out my heart, letting her know I loved her and that I was right there with her, holding her small, fragile hand. I was so close, but the distance between us was a vast canyon.

With shallow breathing and a fragile heartbeat, I could feel her slipping away. And all I could do was watch. Raw feelings surfaced that only I knew. I needed a moment to catch my breath and center myself. Thankfulness, remorse, grief, and love all bubbled to the surface.

My mind wandered, remembering Morgan as a little girl, bouncing around in pigtails, playing dress-up with friends, wearing her "diamonds" to kindergarten, beaming as Mike pinned a corsage on her for the father-daughter dance.

I traveled through time, tracing twenty years of happy memories: carting those crutches across Europe, standing together in awe in the Sistine Chapel, waving as the Pope rolled by in the back of a pickup truck. I was everywhere and nowhere at once, zipping through the plazas of Florence, watching her model a leather jacket, filling out college applications with dreams of a summer abroad, kissing her good night, spending hours in conversation, flying off for a day of shopping on her tenth birthday. Here I was, lying heart to heart with my bright, happy Morgan, a true, loyal friend who always thought of others first and who was never judgmental. That was what set her apart from others, and it was a lesson I could certainly learn from her.

A long procession of friends had come through her hospital room for one last goodbye, a powerful reminder that our daughter loved everyone unconditionally and seemed naturally inclined to light up their world.

Yes, Morgan glowed with a God-given empathetic brilliance, a light that touched us all.

I am tired of crying to you.
Every night my bed is wet with tears;
my bed is soaked from my crying.
—Psalm 6:6

A harsh clatter rose from the carts in the hospital hallway, jolting me back to reality. This was the moment I realized this final goodbye was really happening and that the trip to the hospital was indeed real, not a nightmare after all.

I almost stopped breathing when the nurse came into the room and asked, "Mr. and Mrs. McCarty, is your daughter an organ donor?"

Horror struck every fiber in my being.

Is it time for this?

My instinct kicked in immediately, and my husband and I both said, "No, absolutely not."

"I don't want any medical procedure performed on her," I said, still wanting to protect her from any further harm.

But Kirk pulled me aside. "Mother," he began. "Morgan and I have talked about this. She wanted to be an organ donor, but I guess she never marked it on her driver's license. She knew it would help others."

The time limit was fast approaching, and we had an hour or two to decide. The grueling process was not easy, but focusing on what Kirk had shared with us, Mike and I decided to sign the papers for organ donation. I had a friend at home in Jackson who was waiting for a kidney transplant, and I contacted her immediately to see if she might be a match for Morgan. The lab quickly sent her vital reports, and the team of doctors tested the results. It was not a match.

Then the time arrived.

Our long goodbye was over.

As the organ procurement team circled the room, we were told it was time for the family to go home.

"I will leave this hospital when my daughter leaves," I insisted. "I will stay until the procedure is over."

And that's what we did.

We stayed at the hospital for the next twenty-four hours and waited.

MEANWHILE, THE KNOXVILLE POLICE had been in contact with me about the details of the accident. They had interviewed eyewitnesses who reported that a white vehicle had hit our daughter. Some could identify the person responsible. One witness had been in the car with him that night and told the story to the police. Reportedly, they had attended a party not connected with the UT campus, and they'd gone to get more drugs. Speeding down the campus street, the driver hit Morgan as she was crossing, only a block from her home. He kept driving and did not stop.

Yet they had not been able to find or arrest the driver.

One officer asked, "Can we have your permission to flood the news outlets with her story? We're hoping someone will come forward. I know it will be hard, but this could give us some leads."

We gave permission, and sure enough, every television and radio news program covered the accident, asking for information about a white SUV that had left the scene. The officer said, "We are a close-knit community. We will find who did this."

At that point, I believed him and wanted to bring to justice whoever had done this to Morgan.

When the medical procedure was over, we gathered our devastated family.

We took our baby girl home.

For the last time.

You keep track of all my sorrows.
You have collected all my tears in your bottle.
You have recorded each one in your book.
Psalm 56:8 NLT

9

TRIBUTES

To love and be loved is to feel the sun from both sides.
—David Viscott

On the evening of September 26, 2006, as the sun was setting on a mournful autumn day, Morgan's sorority sisters from Kappa Kappa Gamma held a candlelight memorial vigil on the UT campus. Mike and I had already left Knoxville and returned home to begin preparations for the memorial service that was to be held on September 29, but Ashley (the sorority's chapter president) was thoughtful enough to collect a guest book with attendees' names and their poignant remarks from the campus ceremony. From their accounts of the night and from the newspaper articles, we were comforted by the thoughtful vigil and by how many people came to honor Morgan's life.

The emotional ceremony began with hundreds of friends gathered across Circle Park's greenway. One by one, the candles flickered to life as the attendees sang the chorus of "Amazing Grace."

The vigil drew students, teachers, and friends, many of whom took a turn honoring Morgan with a short statement about what our daughter had meant to them. "Morgan lived life to the fullest," said Ashley, the sorority's chapter president, who was the first to speak as the song ended and the mourners circled around. "Each of these flames represents her life."

One girl who had shared a class with Morgan couldn't believe she was gone. "She was a bright spot in my morning in class with her smile each day."

Close friends spoke about what Morgan's friendship had meant to them, and prayers were said. Many of the participants lingered late into the night, sharing hugs and leaning on each other for support as they shared their own special memories.

One of the girls Jessica said, "I won't walk on campus again without thinking of Morgan. She had a real zest for life. It's hard to think this would happen to someone you know."

But she and the others tried to put those thoughts aside and remember the friend they knew. "Morgan was a lively, talkative friend with a quick laugh and an easy smile," said another sorority sister.

Jennifer Henrick, with whom Morgan had lived, shared, "Morgan would have wanted us to celebrate her life. She always made you smile when you were around her. She introduced me to pretty much everyone I know here. I don't want her memory to ever die away."

Ashley Gilley shared, "The best thing about Morgan being as beautiful and striking as she was on the outside was that she was more beautiful on the inside. That's saying a lot, considering she looked like a supermodel. I am so glad she let Kappa be a part of her life."

~

A Caption in the *Knoxville Sentinel*

> ***Candlelight Vigil: each of these 300 flames represents her life. During this time, three days before the funeral in Jackson, the students had gathered on the University of Tennessee campus.***

~

FOLLOWING THE VIGIL, members of Kappa Kappa Gamma planned to keep Morgan's memory alive by wearing baby blue ribbons in her honor for the rest of the school year. "This is our small way of paying tribute to one of our own, one we all loved," remarked a sorority sister.

The sorority also set up a memorial at the corner of Highland and 17th Street in Knoxville, the intersection where the tragic accident had taken place. Around the sidewalk, they placed a wrought-iron fence holding a black lantern and many flowers, especially blue irises, to represent their sorority. The memorial also included daisies, sunflowers, and beautiful white-and-pink roses, as well as stuffed animals and candles spilling onto the sidewalk. I saw the display months later, and it remained at that corner for almost a year with a sign that read, "In memory of our sister, Morgan McCarty."

MORGAN HAD WORKED part-time at Bella Boutique, so they displayed a blue sash with her name, a blue ribbon, and her picture on the door. That memorial stayed up for the rest of the year. The boutique's hot-pink Christmas tree displayed Morgan's photograph and her jeweled teddy bear. Her coworkers had been like family, and she especially loved the shop's owners, Tom and Kim Buchanan.

Tom and Kim's daughter Tarah had worked with Morgan. "We all loved her so much, and we couldn't wait for her to come to work because she always made us laugh," Tarah said. "She was always thinking of others and would help with my nana's customers when she needed to eat and take a break. Her favorite thing was sorting through the jewelry and rearranging the cases. She was always looking for her next piece to buy, something that suited her cute sense of style, from the newest jewelry that came in straight from New York."

"Morgan had an influence on so many people's lives," Kim added. "I can say she was loved by everyone. I loved her, and I will never forget her." She also revealed that Morgan had set aside a special bracelet with plans to give it to me for my birthday. Kim was thoughtful and generous and gave me the bracelet at the memorial service. This was Morgan's last gift to me, and I will always treasure it.

The day Morgan passed away, the girls clocked her in at work and said, "Now she can never leave because she is clocked in for good. She will always be a Bella girl."

It was comforting to know that so many of Morgan's friends were thinking of her. We had lost our daughter, but they had lost a friend and were hurting too.

We will always cherish that signed guestbook, each attendee offering sincere messages of love and friendship for our daughter. How precious those words have been to me. Morgan's sorority sisters also attended the memorial service in Jackson, sitting together as a group in her honor. They even sang two songs during the service.

I am thankful that Morgan had such close friends to stand beside our family during this tough time, and I'm comforted by knowing they will never forget her.

The important thing is not how many years in your life but how much life in your years.
—Dr. Edward J. Stieglitz

We were contacted by Morgan's sorority to provide input on the new Kappa Kappa Gamma house being built on campus. We had watched the plans evolve since Morgan's freshman year, and we knew it would be a fantastic addition to the University of Tennessee Panhellenic organizations.

At that time, the sorority girls shared one dorm, with each floor housing a different sorority. This new construction would grant each organization their own house and gathering place.

After reviewing several options suggested by the architect, we selected a six-foot, stained-glass window to be placed over the double French doors at the front of the new KKG house. The panes displayed beautiful hues of blue and purple and featured the sorority symbol, a fleur-de-lis, in the center. Many of Morgan's sorority friends, as well as some of my Alpha Delta Pi sorority sisters from college, donated money for the project, designating the window in Morgan's honor. We attended the dedication and opening of the house, where many of the girls from our hometown and from campus came to see the unveiling.

Still today, when we are in Knoxville, we go see "Morgan's window."

"What a lasting tribute to Morgan that will be there for years and generations to come," said the sorority's chapter president.

The bright light that shines through that stained-glass window still carries her radiance over the place where she last lived and loved.

10

GROWING UP IN THE SIXTIES

Some old-fashioned things, like fresh air
and sunshine, are hard to beat.
—Laura Ingalls Wilder

I grew up in a Mayberry-like neighborhood in Jackson. I had loving parents, as well as two sets of adoring grandparents, and I even knew my great-grandparents. My street was full of children whose ages matched those of my sisters and me. In the summer, as soon as the truck hit our neighborhood with its calliope music playing, I would run as fast as the wind to our house for quarters and then chase down the ice cream truck.

"Here it comes!" I would shout at the first sound of the music drifting through the neighborhood, and all of us would run at breakneck speed for our special treats. I could be found with sticky hands from creamy orange Push-Ups or sometimes a Fudgsicle melting down my chin.

My neighborhood playmates and I traveled from backyard to backyard until we got bored, and then the real fun started.

"Let's go to the pond," my sister yelled, and off we would run.

A frog would plop into the water, and butterflies would scatter as we raced to the slippery bank. Tiny fish and crayfish lived just below the surface, and dragonflies skimmed the placid water like tiny planes coming in to land. Discovering see-through tadpoles and dipping minnows from the brownish-green water gave us prizes to show off to our mothers in glorious fruit jars. Oh, the mud! Oh, the mess we made!

"Keep those smelly things outside. Don't bring them in the house," my mother would say as we delivered jars of tadpoles, lizards, and tiny green frogs. Sometimes, we put them in mailboxes to scare the neighbors. Little did we know the mailboxes had holes in the bottoms, and the little creatures would escape soon after we captured them. We thought it would be so cool to have them jump out at the mail carrier the next day.

Never happened, but we always hoped.

Home from the pond, my sisters and I washed off with the garden hose before zooming off for more play. Since we lived in a developing neighborhood, houses were always being built, giving us plenty of intriguing places to explore. Climbing through the frame of a new house, as soon as the construction workers went home in the afternoon, always gave us a chance to find treasures like old pieces of discarded wood or tile pieces.

Our parents warned us to be careful and not play at the construction sites. "Too many loose nails to step on, plus the houses are unfinished and not safe" was the sentiment of all our parents. But the sites were just too tempting, and a few of us always found our way to investigate a new site.

The bonus was if the door was not up yet, we could climb through the boards and play pretend house. Someone would be the mother and pretend to cook in the kitchen, and the younger brothers and sisters would sit in the bathtub, since a tub was always installed early in the construction process. I remember going up the unsteady, not-yet-completed stairway of a house and finding some fabulous pink fluff to jump in.

"Come on!" I shouted to the other kids. "Let's play on the pink pillow rolls in the attic. Look at how cool they are. I bet this will be used in a little girl's room."

"Is it like wallpaper?" one asked.

"No, much too thick," someone reasoned.

"Maybe it goes around the windows. It's a pretty color," all the girls agreed.

"Yeah," everyone chorused, and up the stairs we went, taking turns jumping into the rolling piles of pink fluff.

It didn't take long for all of us to discover this was not a good place to play.

"I'm itching all over," whined Donna, scratching her arms and legs.

"I think it must be from the pink stuff!" I yelled. "Let's get out of here."

Turning and screaming as we ran down the steps, we frantically tried to rub off the fibers, with no luck. Everyone headed home to let our moms figure out what to do.

Turns out we'd discovered pink rolls of wall insulation made of tiny fiberglass threads. When we each ran home, itching and scratching from head to toe, we were directed straight to the bathtub and scolded never to do that again.

Our parents didn't have to tell us twice. That was the worst pile of pink I ever played on. It was even in my hair! "I'm staying away from that part of the houses," I declared, and never did I go near it again.

That was one lesson from my childhood that I never forgot.

11

A MOTHER'S WORK IS NEVER DONE

Be someone's sunshine when their skies are gray.
—Unknown

As a stay-at-home mom, my mother, Louise, was the backbone of our household when we were growing up. My dad sold heavy equipment and traveled during the week. Mother was in charge of our home, caring for three girls on weekdays. Our mother's love and care for her children were never-ending. She took care of me and my two younger sisters, cooked our meals, mowed the lawn, wallpapered, painted, laid sidewalk brick—you name it, she did it.

Mother also made a lot of our clothes, and I don't mean simple things. With the whir of her sewing machine, she could whip out a dress from a Simplicity pattern or make a formal outfit from a twenty-five-piece Vogue pattern in no time. Our favorites were Barbie outfits, ranging from glamorous gowns to bathing suits. She would make our doll clothes without a pattern, relying only on her creativity.

When I was in the ninth grade, we were finally allowed to wear pants to school for the first time.

"I'm so glad to finally be able to wear something other than dresses to school," I said. "But they have rules that the pants and tops must go together, and the tops need to be just above your knees. Where do we get anything like that in our small town? Our dress shops don't have anything like that."

Without blinking an eye, Mother said, "Hancock Fabrics. Go pick out the colors you want, and I'll get a pattern or two for you."

In 1967, double-knit fabric ruled. I got to pick out three or four knit fabrics in avocado green, burnt orange, and mustard yellow. Mother got to work, and the next week I had new outfits to wear to school.

I felt so proud and stylish in my clothes, complete with my Mary Janes from Stegall Shoes at the mall. And the bonus was the fabric didn't even wrinkle!

Wow, what a discovery!

No sewing challenge was too hard for our mother. She once made me a velvet dress with only five days' notice before the homecoming game. Our favorite time for her to sew for us was Halloween. We did not wear store-bought plastic outfits with molded faces. Our very favorite costumes were orange-and-black striped tiger suits complete with hats and ears, gloves and feet. My sister and I loved those outfits and spent hours playing in them long after Halloween was over. Jumping from couch to chair and back again, our tiger leaps were full of scary roars and peals of laughter.

Morgan and Kirk got a chance to wear those costumes for Halloween and played in them for years afterward. Even when Morgan outgrew her tiger suit, she wore Kirk's, which was a bigger size, and continued to enjoy dressing up. Today, I still have those tiger suits, and my granddaughters, the third generation, now love to dress up and play in them. The loud tiger roars continue through the house today. Those costumes were made to last.

Mother continued to sew for Kirk and Morgan after they were born. Her grand labor of love was a beautiful christening gown made when Kirk, the first grandchild, was born. It featured detailed embroidery around the bodice and bonnet; a long, flowing skirt with a slip; beautiful, delicate lace; and tiny pearl buttons down the back. Every grandchild and great-grandchild—for a total of nine so far—has worn that heirloom gown. Carefully preserved for each generation, along with a list of all the babies that have worn it, it is a cherished treasure in our family.

Mother even bought a smocking machine when my kids were little. I would smock the dresses, and she would put them together. We made Kirk a few outfits too, but he soon grew out of the toddler stage. Dresses for every occasion were smocked for Morgan, from Easter bunnies to Christmas scenes with Santa and his reindeer to a first-day-of-school dress with a schoolhouse and school bus. Sixty-one years ago, my mother's faithful Singer sewing machine began stitching up memories that have lasted a lifetime.

My mother also would take turns with the neighborhood mothers by driving carpool to elementary school and junior high. However, unlike the other mothers, she made the drive wearing her brightly flowered housecoat and house shoes. We would load up the blue paneled station wagon, and we never thought she was improperly dressed.

Then she would return home, and the women in the neighborhood would descend on our house for a chat in the breakfast room. Mother would counsel, listen, advise, laugh, and cry as they shared their joys and their problems. By midmorning, after lots of strong coffee and Viceroy cigarettes, the neighborhood wives would disperse back to their homes, and Mother would begin her day. People sought her wise advice and compassion, qualities that drew them to her. She had the ability to see the best in others, just like Morgan.

That was my mother.

She gave me a gift that I did not fully realize until I was grown with children of my own. Mother was never critical or negative with me. Never once. Not that she always agreed with what I did, but I usually came around to her way of thinking. I just couldn't bear to disappoint her in any way.

Later, when I became a mom, I followed Mother's parenting examples with my two children. As they grew, I stayed involved in their lives and chaperoned school and church events, just as my mother had done for me. I never went to a dance without my parents there to help, and I followed in those same footsteps for Morgan and Kirk.

Another example I tried to follow from my parents was that my friends were always welcome at our home. It was not just a fun meeting place for them. It was a safe and happy gathering place for kids of all ages, with a playroom and a vintage jukebox that offered a unique space to socialize. Sleepovers for twenty? No problem. I welcomed Kirk and Morgan's friends into our home, where they were glad to have the basement to themselves. There, they spent countless childhood days watching movies, playing ping-pong, enjoying the pool table, and finding a peaceful place to gather.

In the words of my father, "I never minded the house being full of your friends. I always knew where you were and didn't have to worry about you being gone."

I agreed. One night, the house was full of Morgan's friends while a violent storm brewed outside. Soon, tornado sirens were blaring. It was too dangerous for the kids to drive, so they all called their parents and said they were safe in our basement. The group waited out the storm with popcorn, movies, and lots of laughter.

Our home was a safe haven for Morgan and Kirk's friends, and their presence brought me peace of mind. I understood my dad's encouragement to have friends around. I loved being involved with Kirk and Morgan's friends, just as my parents had been involved with mine. Mother's positive way of parenting had a lasting effect on me and my family, and it still does today in the way we remain involved as loving grandparents.

12

CHILDHOOD PEWS

Count your rainbows, not your thunderstorms.
—Alyssa Knight

It was the quietest moment of the church service. The collection plate was being passed around.

Proud to hold a few coins, I was eager to have a turn to give. As the shiny plate was passed to my small, chubby three-year-old hands, all but one coin made it into the plate. The single coin hit the wooden floor at the back of the church, where we were sitting with my parents, rolled down the slanted planks to the front corner, and then fell into the floor heater register, clinking and clanking all the way to the basement.

I froze in my seat, scared I had done something wrong, when, much to my relief, the minister stood up and said, "Well, that's one quarter we get to keep."

The laughter continued, and then my parents laughed even harder because they knew it was only a dime that I'd dropped.

As a child, I grew up going to church every time the doors were open. My early memories are of wearing the prettiest dresses, most made by my mother, with frilly white petticoats underneath. I wore them with bright white socks and patent-leather shoes.

Our Easter regalia was a whole different story, with preparations for our wardrobe beginning a month or two ahead of time. It was exciting to be dressed from top to toe in new clothes. Our dresses, sometimes matching, were made of voile, dotted Swiss, or frilly organza, with ruffled underpants for my younger sisters and ruffled socks to match. We also wore hats in all shapes and sizes, including the big ones my mother wore, and tiny purses to hold our money. Our final addition to the Easter ensemble was a flower. Dad, who was always spoiling us with flowers, had a tiny corsage for each of us to wear. As we got older, we used roses from our abundant red rose bush at home to adorn our dresses. Add the excitement of full Easter baskets, and it was always one of the most memorable days of the year.

As I GREW UP, another church memory was gathering for picnics at a member's cabin on the Tennessee River. We would pile into the station wagon and travel to the cabin for a day of waterskiing, boat riding, and picnicking—always with fried chicken and deviled eggs on the menu. After a full day of fun, we would gather, tired and a little sunburned from the day on the water, and sing from the Cokesbury hymnal. The small books had all the familiar songs, which so many knew by heart. This was something the entire family looked forward to.

My parents' friends revolved around the church, and so did mine. Our Methodist Youth Fellowship, or MYF, group consisted of members from junior high and high school who stayed close together until we graduated. We made it a point not to miss Sunday night meetings, where we enjoyed games, a meal, a devotional, and were constantly working on fundraisers for the trips we would take.

Our trips were not far from home, but we had no sooner returned from one than we started planning the next. My parents always chaperoned, and my little sisters tagged along. We all learned the value of friendship and community through our church.

Some trips took us to Branson, Missouri, which at that time was a small town, not the touristy city it is today, and to Florida, which we all loved. Nothing to visit or tour there, just the beach for a few days of sun. We also traveled to Atlanta for a Braves baseball game, and we went to

Underground Atlanta for an evening of eating and playing. It was during that trip that my best friend Linda stole my bra and put it in the ice bucket in our room. When I found it, it was frozen stiff. We laughed and laughed, and the memory still makes me smile today.

By the time we got back to our hotel in Atlanta, the pool had already closed for the night. That wasn't going to stop us from having fun. We jumped the fence and enjoyed sitting and talking near the water, that is, until I got thrown into the pool with my clothes on! My screaming woke everyone in the hotel. As the lights came on, we all scattered to our rooms.

WITHOUT A DOUBT, my most devastating trip was to Gatlinburg, Tennessee, which at that time was a small, charming town nestled in the beautiful Smoky Mountains. I was fifteen years old, and on our last day, we were in a chalet on Ski Mountain Road when my dad had a heart attack.

Panic ensued as help was called.

"How can this be? He's only thirty-nine years old," we said.

The ambulance raced up the mountain, and my mother rode with Dad to the nearest hospital. With the siren blaring, the two-lane traffic parted as they sped out of town to the Sevierville hospital. In all the confusion, I ended up staying at the hospital with my parents, while my sisters returned home with our grandparents.

The three of us lived in the hospital room for a week. Mother and I would leave for lunch, and she would let my fifteen-year-old self drive the back-country roads to practice for my license.

Sevierville was the ideal place to practice driving. It was a tiny town, the birthplace of Dolly Parton, with a statue of her in the town square. They barely had a hotel or any place to eat in 1969. It was nothing like the bumper-to-bumper tourist hot spot it is today.

The doctors sent Dad's medical records from Jackson to the doctors in Sevierville, and to his Jackson doctors back home, and they opted not to perform surgery. There was not much damage, but the doctors warned him to cut down on stress.

At that time, he smoked three to four packs of cigarettes a day. Dad always had several farms that he enjoyed working on during the weekends. He had cattle on some with horses, crops on others, hunted on some, and timberland on others. Farmers nearby were hired to take care of the cattle daily and the crops. He was stressed by things going wrong on several of his farms, he was overweight, he worried about our boat, which was constantly being repaired, and he traveled a great deal for his job.

With three young girls, he decided to make some substantial changes in his life.

He quit smoking cold turkey, and so did my mother, who smoked only one pack a day. He went on a diet to lose a few pounds and sold all but one of his farms. Much to our disappointment, the boat was sold to alleviate frustration. No more days on the lake. He cut back on work travel and found himself home more often, which we loved.

With all the changes, his health improved, and those habits bought him precious time. It was twenty-nine years later, at age sixty-eight, that the second attack happened. The second heart attack was major, but Dad recovered and lived eighteen more years.

GROWING UP, church was central to my family life, and I continued this tradition with my own children. Kirk and Morgan participated in youth groups, Christmas pageants, church league basketball and volleyball, camps, trips, choir, and youth retreats. I helped lead the youth group, taught Sunday school classes, and volunteered when needed. Mike helped coach Kirk's basketball team from age six through his senior year in high school. At the same time, he coached Morgan's basketball team and stayed involved until she was a senior also.

One highlight for us was taking part in the nearby Lakeshore Methodist Camp. Our church marked off one weekend a year for the entire family to go to camp with other families.

We did not exactly camp, but we did share a quaint cabin with at least one other family.

We always had lots of kids to play with there, and the hiking, swimming, campfires, and s'mores never seemed to end. It was a special bonding time not only for our family but also for many family friends. The camp offered a wonderful atmosphere, and I'm happy my family enjoyed summers there together.

The church provided a solid foundation for my family, enriching our lives with a sense of community, purpose, and shared values. We made lasting friendships and connections with others with similar beliefs. These moments became cherished family memories, reinforcing values and providing a steady moral compass for our children as they grew into adulthood.

Always remember the commands I give you today. Teach them to your children, and talk about them when you sit at home and walk along the road, when you lie down, and when you get up.
—Deuteronomy 6:6–7

13

DYNAMITE DAD

A good laugh is sunshine in the house.
—William Makepeace Thackeray

When I was about eight, Dad bought us two Shetland ponies that we loved and kept at our grandparents' house, which was close to our home. The older pony, Star, was broken, but the younger one was not, and Dad thought we could fix that problem. Star had a white patch on his nose shaped like a star, along with a golden mane and tail. The other pony was white with black spots, so we named him Patches.

One day, as I was riding Star, my dad got the idea of putting my little sister Donna on the smaller pony for a quick ride. An unbroken pony, regardless of its size, is not a pleasant thing to encounter. Patches took off with Donna screaming at the top of her lungs. Sure enough, she was thrown from the saddle in tears.

I rushed to help her up, asking, "Are you okay?"

She brushed off her new clothes, crossed her arms, and didn't answer. Instead, she let our father know exactly what she was thinking. "Dad, why did you put me on this pony? He's the bad one! I'm never getting back on him again."

"I didn't think Patches had it in him to buck you off," Dad said as he checked Donna for injuries.

Just because Donna was small didn't mean the pony wouldn't notice someone trying to ride him, I thought, as I sized up the situation.

"I'm so sorry, sweetie," Dad told Donna. "I'm glad you weren't hurt. This pony is far too ornery for you girls. I'll just leave this one out in the pasture. No more riding Patches."

Once again, I sized up his parenting skills. How could he think a four-and-a-half-year-old could break a pony?

Dad gathered the ponies and led them both to the barn.

Lesson learned by Dad: we were not cowgirls, and this was not a rodeo.

That was just *one* of the dangerous things we did with my dad.

My dad, though often away during the workweek, made up for it on the weekends. Hunting and hanging out on the farm were his hobbies, and since my tomboy sister, Kandy, was the only one who would hunt with him, I spent my time there fishing in ponds and riding our horses.

Our fun farm adventures continued, and some of my favorite memories involved beavers. They would dam up the creek on Dad's farm and flood the forest land. The solution? Blow up the dams with dynamite! We couldn't wait to help.

Dad, because of his road-building job, had access to dynamite that was used occasionally on his sites. He would let us ignite the fuse and *BAM!* An explosion of sticks, logs, and rocks would skyrocket into the air as we jumped up and down, cheering.

"Let me do it first! I'm the oldest," I would yell, as Dad set the fuse and then let me ignite it. Then we would wait and count down to the big explosion.

FIVE, FOUR, THREE, TWO, ONE!

BOOM! BAM!

I would scream as the water and timber exploded into the air, and then the water would start to break free.

After a second blast, which my sister, Donna, would manage, the water would flow freely downstream, just like it was supposed to do. The natural boundaries of the creek would fill into place, and the water would return to its original riverbed.

However, the industrious beavers took only a week or two to rebuild a perfect dam of sticks and logs right where the last beaver mound had stood.

I learned firsthand the meaning of the saying, *busy as a beaver.*

"I'm amazed at how fast they work. We were just here a few weeks ago, and the spring was clear, and water was flowing," I shouted when we arrived at the site and discovered the land was flooded yet again.

It was a vicious cycle of man versus wildlife.

The wildlife always won.

ANOTHER ACTIVITY DAD enjoyed was taking us out on our ski boat to nearby Piney Lake on weekends. I always looked forward to being out on the crystal-blue water, swimming while Mother packed our red plaid picnic basket, which she'd acquired with S&H Green Stamps from the local Piggly Wiggly grocery store. Crispy fried chicken was always a must, along with pimento cheese sandwiches, deviled eggs, and Charlie Chips in a huge five-gallon can delivered to our house each week. Cookies and gallons of lemonade came to the rescue as we left the water's edge, thirsty from our swim. Since my sisters were four and eight years old, they would play on rafts and go boarding.

"Dad made the best board ever," I would tell my friends, as we enjoyed many weekends being pulled behind the boat, laughing and having fun. The board would glide across the water, attached to the back of the boat with ski ropes. It was about six feet long, painted royal blue, with a rounded front and a mat attached in the middle. A heavy, fat rope was used to hold on for dear life as the board swung out over the wake on the smooth water.

Our board was much larger than the two-person boards you see today. Ours had the ability to hold five or six people at a time, and that is where the fun began. Of course, the last one on the board would be the first one to go soaring off at top speed, tumbling through the air before coming back for more.

My best friend, Linda, was always with us, riding the waves and yelling, "Slow down!" as we giggled and held the rope, trying not to fall off.

The best time was late in the afternoon, when the lake would calm, and the water would become slick as glass. The board could really glide, and all I could do was hang on.

If you were really seasoned, you could stand and hold the rope, waving as if in a parade. My sisters, Donna and Kandy, would lie on their stomachs and glide in all directions over the still water. I liked piling onto the board with Linda and zooming around the lake for a quick exit. I also skied on my old-fashioned wooden Cypress Gardens water skis, but boarding was always my favorite way to enjoy the lake.

Friends built a ski chair, which consisted of an aluminum chair bolted to buoys and long ropes attached to the ski boat. Not the prettiest thing on the lake, but anybody—and I mean anybody—could ride around the lake on the ski chair. If you could sit up, you could enjoy the ski chair. While this offered no challenge for us girls, it provided lots of entertainment for the adults. This led to plenty of laughter as our mothers tried not to get their weekly beauty-shop hairstyles wet while riding the ski chair.

Weary by the end of the day, I would drive the boat onto the trailer. Then an exhausted group of sunburned girls and our parents would head home, picnic basket empty and many happy memories in tow.

MY DAD, a college history major, loved to educate his three girls with in-depth lessons, especially on vacation. All we three girls ever wanted to do was drive to Florida for a week and play at the beach, but he would have none of that.

"There's nothing educational to see at the beach," he would say. Then would come our moaning and groaning, but nothing could change his mind.

We first traveled close to home when my sisters were small, and we were able to visit every national park and landmark in the seven states surrounding Tennessee. Piling into my dad's shiny new company car, off we would go, with both our parents smoking cigarettes like smokestacks. Heaven knows how much smoke and nicotine we inhaled because the car windows were always shut for the air conditioner. With no laws regarding safety belts or car seats for children at that time, I claimed the window side of the back seat; Donna, the second oldest, claimed the other side; and Kandy, the youngest, sometimes got the rear window ledge, where she would sprawl out with her pillow. Thank goodness that, for all our traveling, we had no accidents with Kandy in the back window!

Bored as we were, there were some exciting moments—like the time I was almost mauled by a black bear.

In the sixties, the bear population in the Smokies was plentiful and very visible to tourists. I remember stopping at a popular overlook. Where people gathered, bears often did too. Sure enough, we saw bears wandering from car to car, searching for handouts of food.

My dad wanted to get a picture of me with a bear, so I got out of the car, and a huge black bear decided to stroll over to check me out. The picture taken on my dad's instant Polaroid camera showed my body turning to run, panic on my face, and my hair in a perfect spiral, twirling around my head as I leaped back into the car.

"Are you trying to get me mauled?" I screamed as I slammed the door behind me. "That bear was so close I could smell his musky fur and feel his hot breath! I was almost attacked!"

"Don," my mother said sternly, "that was too close. I don't think we need any more pictures. We see all the bears just fine from the safety of our car."

"Look!" I screamed as I threw up my hands. "The bear is now on the hood of our car for a better look at us."

The curious bear had crawled onto the hood and was peering at us through the windshield. Pawing at the glass, he grew discouraged when he could not get in, and then he rolled off the car like a toddler. After hitting the pavement, off he went to investigate other interesting cars.

We all agreed that was not the safest way to take a picture.

"I think we could just buy a postcard of the black bears next time and not have to endanger anyone's life," said my mother.

Dad showed that photograph to friends and family for years because he loved telling the story about his daughter and the black bear. We also got pictures of bears on the hood of our car and by the windows. The curious bears did not understand why we weren't feeding them. Because so many people did, the bears got to be dangerous and aggressive.

Eventually, the park rangers moved a feeding station deep into the forest, hoping to keep the bears away from the hordes of photo opportunists. It was a good idea for the safety of the bears and the tourists, but as a child, I was disappointed to no longer see such large numbers of bears when we visited the mountains.

Today, they are not the aggressive bears I remember from the sixties. When I visit Great Smoky Mountains National Park now, I usually see them with their cubs foraging for berries or looking down from trees. Most keep their distance from people instead of looking for handouts. That keeps everyone safer.

Continuing our educational vacations, we visited the three Tennessee homes of US presidents: The Hermitage in Nashville, home of Andrew Jackson; Andrew Johnson's home in Greenville; and James K. Polk's home and museum in Columbia.

Our Tennessee history was getting high marks as Dad checked off his educational list.

The state wasn't finished until we saw Lookout Mountain and Rock City in Chattanooga. The Fairyland Caverns were perfect for kids, with tiny trolls and stories all throughout the Mother Goose Village.

Two of my favorite attractions were the Fat Man's Squeeze walkway, through which we had to walk sideways through the narrow stone gap, and the swinging rope bridge to Lover's Leap. From that lookout, we could see seven states, which, of course, we had to identify—Tennessee, Kentucky, Virginia, South Carolina, North Carolina, Georgia, and Alabama.

"Looks like a lot of trees and mountains to me," I said to my sister, who giggled in agreement.

I was amazed that so many states looked alike. Thank goodness the markers told us where to look, or I would have been confused for sure. Mother agreed.

Next, we journeyed to Shiloh National Military Park along the Tennessee River. During the scariest part of the tour, I shuddered when we passed the Bloody Pond. The two-day 1862 Civil War battle saw 24,000 Union and Confederate casualties, and some of the dead ended up near that pond, a fact that haunted me as a child.

We also visited Mammoth Cave in nearby Kentucky, reportedly the world's longest cave system. I remember lots of bats, which both thrilled and terrified me.

On other trips, we toured historic Hot Springs National Park in Arkansas, the US Space & Rocket Center in Huntsville, Alabama, and Stone Mountain Park in Georgia near Atlanta.

All these historical and educational trips did not impress my two sisters or me in the least. Sure, we did have fun, but our hearts were somewhere else, like on a beach.

FINALLY MY SISTERS were getting a little bigger, and we could venture to other parts of the country.

"Yippee!"

Dad decided to broaden our travels and head out West.

I couldn't wait to see the sights.

"Dad, I can't believe we are still seeing historical sites. Can we just get a break for a change?"

"Who goes to these places, like the Dwight D. Eisenhower Presidential Library and Museum in Abilene, Kansas?" I asked.

"We do," Dad said proudly. "It's broadening your educational travel in the United States."

He still had stops meant strictly for learning: the Cherokee Heritage Center in Oklahoma, the state of Nebraska for a stop on the Oregon Trail, and every state capital of the states we traveled through. The

Rocky Mountain National Park and Pikes Peak were a treat because we stayed in cozy cabins near a babbling creek outside Colorado Springs. They had fireplaces and no central heat, so we piled brightly colored blankets on our beds at night to stay warm.

"I'll bring the firewood in, and maybe we can roast marshmallows tonight," Dad said.

I played in the creek outside our cabin until dark. It reminded me of the Little Pigeon River in the Smokies, as it flowed and bubbled down the mountains. The frigid mountain stream became a perfect playground as we waded and jumped from rock to rock, trying not to get wet.

"Remember, there are grizzly bears in these mountains," Mother warned. "We don't want to be out past dark."

We piled into our wooden cabin, where Mother made a picnic supper with the supplies we had picked up at the store on the way—ham and cheese sandwiches, Fritos, Twinkies, and brownies with icing. Dad retrieved the drinks from the stream, where our Cokes and Dr Peppers had become icy cold. A perfect feast for tired, worn-out campers. We did not have to be rocked to sleep that night.

After Colorado, we went to Cheyenne, Wyoming, just so my dad could get a Stetson cowboy hat. He was thrilled to buy one from the store that he had mail-ordered from back at home in Tennessee. We had planned to visit national parks in several other states, including the Grand Canyon and Yellowstone, but we got a call from home that Grandfather Kirk was critically ill and in the hospital. Our trip ended that day, and we hurried back to Tennessee.

Even having to cut our trip short, it was the best vacation we'd had so far.

FINALLY WHEN I GRADUATED from high school, we planned a Florida beach trip with my aunt, uncle, and cousin Jay.

"Hallelujah!" I cheered. "I can't believe Dad finally caved in and let us have a real vacation! He must be getting soft in his old age."

"It only took twelve years to get to the ocean," echoed Donna.

I had been to Florida several times with friends and youth groups, but never with the entire family.

My sisters were as thrilled as I was, since we all wanted an escape from our normal educational destinations. Piling into the car and claiming our backseat positions, off we went for sun and sea.

Each day, we frolicked in the water from morning until evening, and then we dragged our tired selves to the hotel pool for a night swim. It was a glorious stay without one historical or educational site—not even a state capital.

My dad thought it was a complete waste of our time, although he did enjoy the bounty of fresh shrimp, grouper, and crab each night.

As an adult, I now have quite a different view of our family vacations. Thanks to Dad's determination to educate us, I've visited forty-seven of the fifty states. If my sisters and I had had our way, we would have spent every summer at the same beach and never would have had the privilege of seeing our beautiful country.

What a gift, even though I didn't recognize the importance of his wisdom at the time. Now, I cherish those family experiences, and I share the love of travel he bestowed on all of us as we grew up. Dad knew what he was doing. He put up with all our eye rolls, whining, and fussing about his historical destinations and never wavered in his desire to show us the country. Thanks, Dad, for instilling the travel bug in all of us.

The wanderlust continued with both Kirk and Morgan taking school trips to New York and Washington, DC when they each turned twelve. During our own family vacations, we visited many different states and even toured Europe. Morgan enjoyed Broadway plays, and every few years, we would go on girls' trips to see the latest plays and shop in New York City.

Yes, Dad, I learned from you that travel could be both fun and educational. You would be proud of all the exciting places we have taken Kirk and Morgan.

But there was one lesson that didn't stick.

Much to your disapproval, our family still goes to the beach each year.

14

GOD'S HANDS

Even the darkest night will end and the sun will rise.
—Les Misérables, the musical

Many people I know have had a faith crisis in their lives. From the drug revolution infiltrating families to random acts of violence, alcohol misuse, and domestic abuse, the breakdown of families can cause anyone to seek a higher authority for help. We did not have to face a similar situation until we got our wake-up call in 1998, when Morgan developed an eating disorder at thirteen years of age.

Morgan had broken her arm practicing a back handspring for cheerleading tryouts and was out of physical activity while she healed. This was a big change from the busy schedule she normally maintained with sports and after-school activities. She began to gain weight from inactivity, and she did not like it. On her own, she started cutting back on her food intake.

"You look great," her friends told her over and over when Morgan started losing weight. Since she received compliments everywhere she went, the attention became a reward of sorts, and her weight-loss journey continued, even when she did not need to lose any more weight.

I was a little concerned, but she was still eating meals with the family, so I thought it was under control. Little did I know that was the farthest thing from the truth.

Morgan was caught in a downward spiral reinforced by the compliments. She was eating fewer calories each day and continued to lose weight.

By the second month, her clothes were hanging off her, so I told her, "Morgan, this has got to stop. You need to listen not just to me, but to a medical doctor. There are real dangers in what you are doing to yourself."

At this point, I took her to her doctor to get some help.

Unfortunately, the doctor said, "You're at the lower end of the weight range for your height of five feet ten inches, but you're not in danger." He went on to talk to her about the importance of eating healthy and nutritious foods, and that was that.

No help there.

I left feeling as if the doctor had approved of her weight loss, as if he too had complimented her on the results of her poor eating habits.

Of course, Morgan made no change in her eating habits following that visit.

While everyone else kept telling her how beautiful she looked, my fears continued to grow. I felt I was losing control of her as she withered away.

First, she cut out snacks. Then she would opt for smaller meal portions. Finally, she stopped eating dinner at home with the family, insisting she wasn't hungry.

I would get her to eat occasionally, but nothing like the daily meals we'd always shared. In my heart, I knew this was not just some little phase she was going through. This was becoming a serious issue, and I was in a panic.

By month three, she went camping with her youth group. I warned the counselors, "Morgan has become a picky eater, so don't be alarmed."

I hoped the campout would help her revert to her healthy eating habits by giving her extended time with friends in a social setting.

"I'm sending energy bars and a few snacks," I told the counselors, knowing they would not be used to her finicky eating habits.

When they returned from the two-day retreat, the youth director asked to talk to me privately.

In a concerned tone, she warned, "I'm worried that Morgan has a serious eating problem. She skipped all but one of the meals this weekend. The telling factor was that she knew the exact calorie count in the foods and refused to eat anything if she didn't know exactly what was in it. She would talk about the food, but she wouldn't eat any. I'm worried about her health. I'm also concerned that other girls might follow her example because she's a leader in the group."

I thanked the youth director for her genuine concern and honesty.

"I've been worried about her too, but I guess I just kept hoping it would go away with time," I said, blinking back tears. "You've opened my eyes to the seriousness of this problem."

Morgan had always been a happy, confident, beautiful girl, so these new behaviors had shocked me to the point of denial, especially with so many friends and even the doctor assuring me all was fine. While I was in constant turmoil over it, I had been struggling to accept that her picky eating had really gone this far. Maybe I didn't want to see how far it had gone. But the conversation with the youth director became a turning point for me. Now, there was no more denying the severity of this problem.

At a loss for how to help Morgan, I knew this battle would be an uphill climb. I finally began to accept that Morgan was suffering from an eating disorder. This was serious.

The next few weeks can only be described as a nightmare. Morgan denied any problem, which is typical, of course. She became a recluse, staying in her room and withdrawing from family, friends, and the world around her.

"Honey, I need you to listen to me," I begged. "You're ruining your health and throwing away your life."

"Mother, I'm just not hungry," she argued, pulling away from me. "Just let me go rest," and off she'd go, back to cocoon again in her room.

Her personality had changed from her normally outgoing, bubbly energy to a quiet girl who was avoiding social interaction. These were not traits I had ever seen in Morgan. Her thoughts and actions were all about her looks now, and she had become fixated on maintaining control of her body. I would often find her curled up in a ball in her bed, exhausted, her arms wrapped around herself to keep warm.

Sadly, all my begging and pleading weren't helping, and eventually pushed her away. I tried to entice her by making her favorite foods, but to no avail.

Her constant reply was "I'm not hungry."

One afternoon, I got her to eat some homemade brownies, but much to my dismay, she would not eat anything else the rest of the day. She began to wear baggy clothes to hide her thin body. Her body fat had dropped so low that she could no longer regulate her body temperature. She learned to cover her tracks if I asked what she had eaten that day. It was usually more drinks than food, with little more than bars or crackers sustaining her. I usually got the irritated reply, "I'll eat when I get hungry, not now."

At that time in 1998, there was no information about eating disorders available anywhere in our hometown. We had no local counselors or clinics to turn to for help, but I knew of one family who had successfully dealt with their daughter's eating disorder. I reached out, and her mother said her daughter was doing much better after receiving professional counseling at Vanderbilt University Medical Center in Nashville.

I called and got an appointment, but it was still two weeks away.

Meanwhile, things were getting worse. Morgan's size 0 clothes were now too big, and she was beginning to look like a lanky scarecrow.

Still people kept complimenting her, which continued to reinforce her unhealthy behavior. I wanted to scream each time she was told how good she looked. Couldn't they see we had a serious battle going on here? Were people blind to what was happening?

As the mother, I was used to fixing things for my family, especially for my children. If she had suffered a more common illness, I could have gotten her treatment or found medicine for her. But anorexia does not have a quick cure, and the possibility of her healing herself was not feasible.

This all happened in a matter of two to three months, and I was left feeling helpless, afraid, and broken. I had asked a few friends for prayer because praying was all there was left for me to do. Our family had been turned upside down in such a short period of time, and we were losing

Morgan. Mike and Kirk also tried to encourage her to eat. They got the same response from her: "Just leave me alone."

One afternoon, Morgan wanted to attend a youth rally at a local college to meet other friends from churches around our conference area. I dropped her off, and I will never forget the feeling of helplessness that suddenly descended over me.

As I drove off, I started crying out of frustration. I released such deep sobs that I had to pull the car over. Behind the wheel, I raised my voice and threw my hands in the air, "God, why is this happening to Morgan? I have done all that I can possibly do." Through my tears, I begged, "Morgan needs help. I am turning her over to you, God. I ask you to heal this eating disorder in her mind and body."

I had never done anything like that before, but as I drove home, I continued praying for a miracle. Giving up control of your child is a scary thing, but I had done all I could do to help her.

When I went back to pick her up from the rally that afternoon, Morgan got into the car and said, "Mother, I saw a girl from the Memphis group who was skin and bones from being anorexic. She looked terrible, and I don't want to end up like that. I'll do what you want me to do to get better."

An answer to my prayer! I felt an instant burden lift off my shoulders. I couldn't believe my ears. This was the first time she had acknowledged that she really wanted to get better.

She was willing to get help. This was no small miracle.

I rejoiced and thanked God for this admission—a critical turning point in her recovery journey.

It took many months of going back and forth to appointments in Nashville, requiring a little prodding each time, but she was committed to getting better and began to change her compulsive behavior. Her eating improved. She began branching out and eating a variety of foods, and sitting down for family meals again. Not big portions, but eating with us instead of escaping into her room alone.

We were thrilled and relieved that she was joining the family at the table again. Her normal personality slowly started to come back as her unhealthy habits disappeared. But it took longer to rid her mind of the compulsive thoughts. The mirror had become the enemy, making her think she wasn't thin enough. Months went by before I could say we had our old Morgan back again, not the shell of a girl who had been consumed by body image. She still had a few foods she considered off limits, but slowly she returned to a healthy weight for her height, and she began to be content with herself again.

Her Vanderbilt doctor said, "Two things helped in her recovery. Her young age and the fact that she was willing to come for help without resistance. Consent is a major part of accepting treatment. The patient must want to change."

Sadly, he also told me that many people in their later teens and adulthood never recover from eating disorders. We were one of the lucky ones to have had only a brief brush with this horrific disease of the mind.

What the doctor did not know is the role God played in healing Morgan's spirit, mind, and body. "He descended on Morgan that day at the youth rally," I told Mike through grateful tears.

God's Hands. God's healing grace. Nothing else could have changed her attitude in a few hours' time.

Thanks to that answered prayer, Morgan was back.

LORD, ***my God, I prayed to you,***
and you healed me.
—Psalm 30:2

15

PARENTING THE PARENT

Let the warm glow of the setting sun kiss life's hurts away.
—Unknown

I have grieved many deaths in my family, each in a different way—Morgan, with an untimely, traumatic death, and my mother, with the long goodbye, a journey through seven years of suffering from Alzheimer's.

My mother, Louise, was vivacious and outgoing, and her three daughters were the love of her life. A wonderful role model, she guided us without condemnation and was there for us through childhood and into adulthood. Despite severe rheumatoid arthritis as she aged, not much could keep her down. Once the five-foot-one former captain of her high school basketball team, she later used a motorized chair to get around, but her spirit remained strong. She could still play bridge, board games, and the piano, all of which brought her great joy. Then, as the years passed, she slowly lost the ability to remember our names.

Mother was widely admired for her musical gifts. Once, a friend of her brother Bob's, who was stationed overseas, called her during a bout of homesickness.

"Mrs. Louise," he said, "I need a bit of cheering up. Just ten minutes can shake the blues, and nobody can play that piano like you can. Would you please play some boogie-woogie?"

"Sure, I will!" Laughing, my mother went straight to the piano and played for the lonely soldier, eager to bring him a little piece of home. People near and far were drawn to my mother's outgoing personality, as well as her warmth and charm.

For the first five years of her illness, Mother was cared for at home with help from a daily caretaker, Clara. Each afternoon and evening, my dad took over. He learned to do things for her—and around the house—that he had never done before she became ill. Cooking and laundry were the biggest adjustments. Yet he tackled those duties without a single complaint.

"See? You really can teach an old dog new tricks," he would say. He had never even turned on the washing machine or the oven before, but he took pride in his growing efficiency around the house.

After Mike and I got married, we lived down the street from my parents. That enabled our children to spend lots of quality time with their grandparents by just riding their bikes down for a visit. As my mother's health worsened and she could no longer get out much, Kirk and Morgan spent hours with her, playing board games like Aggravation and her favorite, Yahtzee.

I learned firsthand that having a family member whose memory is failing is a challenge. My mother grew upset when she forgot simple things, like the names of close friends and loved ones. My sisters and I were upset watching our mother lose her mental capacity. My dad was upset as she continued to spiral downward, having only a few good days every month.

The situation wasn't going to be sustainable for much longer. We all knew that, eventually, we would have to make an executive decision and seriously consider long-term care options. But we were hoping to keep her at home for as long as possible.

She'd been declining for about five years when Dad had to undergo carotid artery surgery. His doctor warned him not to lift anything for a few weeks after the surgery, which made his caregiving duties particularly challenging.

I had stopped by to check on them, as I did most afternoons, and found them sitting together under the sprawling sweetgum tree in their front yard. When Dad stood up to greet me, I was shocked to see blood spilling from his neck bandages and running down his shirt.

Dad didn't panic. In fact, he hadn't even known he was bleeding. "All I did was lift the wheelchair into the yard," he said casually.

"You've broken open your stitches," I said with my hands on my hips. "What were you thinking? You're not supposed to lift anything."

All my worst fears began to surface. I had long been worried that taking care of my mother was too much for Dad, but now I was convinced that it was killing him.

"This is too much for you to manage by yourself. I know we've been avoiding any care placement, but today is THE DAY."

At that, I got in the car and went straight to the long-term-care facility. It wasn't just time to get more help for our mother. It was past time.

I was relieved to learn there would be a room available for her to move into on Monday. We just had to make it through the weekend.

So I took care of the paperwork, dreading the trip home to tell my family the news.

"It's done," I told my dad. "It will be the best thing for you both."

Teary-eyed and defeated, he reluctantly agreed.

Through more tears, my sisters also reconciled themselves to the fact that moving Mother to the long-term-care memory center would be the best solution for both of our parents. As hard as it was to do, we all felt confident that she would be well cared for in this facility, and she was.

The greatest fear came on Monday, when it was time to move her out of her home. We were afraid she would realize where she was going and protest the move.

Holding our breaths, we were shown to a room and got her settled. Thankfully, she was calm and pleasant. She greeted the nurses and staff as we explained to her that she would be staying for a while and that they would be taking care of her. Not missing a beat, she remained her charming and polite self.

"Everyone seems nice," she commented.

My two sisters, Dad, and I had a good cry on the way home. Even though she hadn't realized she was being placed in a care facility, leaving her there was so hard—another stage of letting go of our mother and a difficult grief in its own way. Still, we all knew this decision was for the best.

We were all relieved to give our father a chance to return to being a husband instead of a full-time caregiver. Dad now had the freedom to come and go as needed, but he was at her bedside for all three meals each day, lavishing on her the love and attention she rightly deserved. Fresh flowers were placed in her room each week, and we brought candy and special treats to brighten her days.

Mother thrived at the facility. She gained a few pounds and adjusted to her new routines, never questioning where she was or asking about home.

That was a tremendous relief and blessing for our family.

Her health continued to decline over the last two years of her life. Eventually, she did not recognize anyone but Dad. His devotion and love for her were never shown more brightly than on a stormy, tornado-warned night. High winds caused trees to fall, and some roads were closed because of obstructions. He called to tell me, "I'm heading out to check on your mother."

"Dad, it's eleven o'clock," I argued. "The doors will be locked, and besides, it's not safe to be out in this weather."

"I just want to be with her," he said. "I think the electricity is off, and she might be frightened."

"You'll be risking your life getting out in this horrible weather. Where are your good senses?" I said. "Besides, Mother won't know whether you are there or not."

"Yes," he said calmly. "But I will know."

How could I possibly argue with that?

I said not another word, and off he went to comfort his beloved wife through the storm. He sat there with her, side by side in the dark, holding her hand until the lights came back on and the danger was over.

I will never forget that night nor the lesson of commitment and steadfast love. My parents were sharing their own version of *The Notebook*, showing us how love really can endure all things.

Do not reject me when I am old;
do not leave me when my strength is gone.
—Psalm 71:9

I had said goodbye to my mother three years earlier, when she could no longer recognize me. Then I vanished from her memory completely. What a cruel disease, to take her mind, her memories, and her family from her. She had always been such a strong, independent woman, and she would have been horrified to know others had to care for her in her final years.

But we considered it a privilege to care for Mother through her decline. She had been such a role model, a source of love and support, and a blessing to my sisters and me. She radiated love and warmth to her grandchildren with every embrace.

One mercy was that she never knew Morgan had died. By then, she no longer recognized her family, and we did not want to confuse or upset her.

I would have given anything to have been able to turn to my mother during that terrible season. Thankfully, my dad, my sisters, and Mike were there for me, and I was grateful. But there is nothing like having your mother by your side. After Morgan died, I longed for my mother's wisdom and comfort.

She was the best mother in every way, and she is still deeply missed by all who loved her. I can still hear her saying, "I don't want you to worry about me. I'll be just fine."

Mother lived to be eighty years old.

She was selfless to the end.

A life well lived, but a long goodbye.

16

THE FOREVER GRIEF

Ain't no sunshine when she's gone.
—Bill Withers

For the first days and even weeks after losing someone, you have the feeling of living in a fog. Everything is disorienting. When grief strikes unannounced, your body another dimension. Memory doesn't function properly. Thinking logically is an issue. Whole blocks of time are lost, as are the details of what is happening around you.

When Morgan died, my thoughts seemed muffled, and my actions became mechanical. It was as if I were looking down at myself, watching myself live someone else's life.

I just had to endure.

Endure the questioning of my faith.

Endure the suffocating loneliness.

Endure the self-imposed isolation.

"I can't think or make important decisions," I told my husband. I knew I was not working with a clear mind, so I relied on friends to help us make even simple choices.

Overcome with grief, I complained to my sister, "I'm angry! My family was destroyed so quickly, with no warning. How can anyone prepare for something like this?"

I wanted to escape. I did not want to accept my life with so much sorrow and pain.

Escape sounded good.

In *A Grief Observed*, C. S. Lewis examines the perplexity of grief: "No one ever told me that grief felt so like fear."

After losing his wife, Joy, Lewis writes about anger, fear, doubt, and the depths of pain. His grief was not easy or pretty. Lewis showed that his path was clouded by fear and doubt until the sun finally broke through the darkness.

When Morgan died, I felt that darkness.

People reached out to us, but even their loving touch did little to fill the emptiness in my aching heart. The pain of my deep loss was indescribable. Losing a child is simply not the natural order of things. There is no common name for parents who lose a child. It is not supposed to happen. If you lose a spouse, you are a widow or widower. If you lose your parents, you are an orphan. But we have no word to name the unnatural loss of a child or a sibling.

Of course, where there is deep grief, there is also great love. Grief and love are two sides of the same coin. The more deeply we love someone, the greater the pain we feel when that person is gone.

The people who helped us the most were other parents who had lost a child. Somehow, they were still living and breathing, even years after their loss. Their resilience gave me hope, and I clung to the fact that they had survived. If they had learned to live in the wake of such great loss, maybe, just maybe, we could too.

When I turned to these families for guidance, they suggested I go easy on myself. "Try to take it one day at a time," one friend said. "Or even one hour at a time. Make a goal to do one thing each day. Get dressed. Take a shower. Eat a meal. Start small."

Another friend shared, "Don't worry about getting back to normal. It will take a while. Go at your own pace. You have a new normal now, so prepare yourself for holidays and birthdays. They will be bumps in the road, but, you have to prepare for the hard days ahead."

Their advice was wise and gentle, and Mike and I listened. These were friends who knew what we were going through. They understood our pain.

"I am relying on you to guide me through this horrible time in our lives," I told them, for they had endured the same horrific loss of their own children.

Normally an avid reader, I could barely read a paragraph at a time after Morgan died. My focus vanished. I nodded during conversations but absorbed nothing and felt empty behind my smile.

My eyes stared blankly at the news, but nothing sank in. Meeting other couples who had experienced similar loss reassured us that what we were facing was normal, and their stories comforted us by showing us that there could be survival beyond grief.

Our close circle of friends, family, and church community took care of us as we came home after Morgan's final days. We were overwhelmed by the kindness extended to us during that week. While we were in Knoxville and unable to be home for a few days, friends asked us if they could get the house ready.

"Go ahead," we said. Little did we know that dozens of people would descend on our house, organizing food, straightening up, mowing our yard, and they even cleaned out our refrigerator.

By the time we arrived home from Knoxville, we were emotionally exhausted but wanted to see Mike's mother and my father, who had not been with us at the hospital, as well as Mike's sisters from Florida. They were a big comfort, and they helped us start planning the memorial service for later that week.

They told us when to eat, when to sleep, and what to do during those days. We couldn't have managed even the simplest decisions without caring friends and family guiding us. With our brains in a fog, we were happy to have help.

It was like we were on a roller coaster in the dark, unable to see the dips, turns, or changes in direction. It was an out-of-control feeling, filled with numbness and fear.

I learned that people grieve in different ways, and that is all right. I wanted to be around friends and loved ones. Their company and support comforted me. My goal was not to be left alone, especially at first. I couldn't trust myself to make clear decisions.

My husband, on the other hand, wanted to grieve alone. That was his personality. Where I reached out, he withdrew, and he needed the space and time to process his sorrow internally, away from the crowds of people who surrounded our family with love and care.

For example, our first holiday came soon after Morgan's passing. That Thanksgiving was miserable for all of us. But as we gathered with extended family, Mike felt too boxed in, while I was grateful to be surrounded by loved ones. It was a matter of personality, and either way was understandable.

Some people do anything they can to avoid the pain, choosing to ignore grief rather than face it. Most people find that whether you grieve now or ten years from now, you must go through the process at some point. You will never "get over it." Grief stays with you all your life. It will never completely go away because you will always have that memory with you.

In my experience, grief has levels of intensity, and you learn how to the waves as the years go on.

Grief is the last act of love we give to our loved one. Where there is deep grief, there was great love.
—Robert Orr

A friend who had experienced great loss, warned me. "People will turn away from us in grocery stores to avoid talking to us," she said.

I thought that wouldn't happen to me, but it did. Repeatedly.

Sometimes I saw people pushing their carts in the opposite direction to avoid coming face-to-face with me. I knew those people just didn't know what to say. Avoiding an encounter was the easiest way out of an uncomfortable situation.

Still, it hurt. Every time.

During my first trip out of the house by myself, I wore sunglasses in case I got weepy going up and down the grocery aisles. I needed a shield between the public and my tears. Sure enough, between seeing Morgan's favorite chocolate brownies and running into someone who had not heard about our loss and innocently asked about the family, I was a crying mess. With sunglasses to the rescue, I wheeled out of

Kroger as fast as I could. I would have to finish my shopping another day.

From my own experiences, I try not to avoid others in a comparable situation. Instead, I simply smile, give a hug, or say, "I'm thinking of you and your family." Simply acknowledging someone's loss head-on rather than ignoring them can be powerful, as well as comforting to the person who is grieving. It takes a lot for that person to be out of the house in public, especially in those early days, and a quick recognition of their pain and grief is often a reassurance that you care.

I want people to know that losing a child is not contagious.

Be the friend who lifts someone up instead of the one who pulls away.

Dr. James Moore's book, *When Grief Breaks Your Heart*, recognizes these six stages of grief: numbness, anger, loneliness, questioning, guilt, and acceptance.

One thing I've learned is that grief is not a linear process.

You will not go straight through the stages in order. You might be stuck in one phase for weeks or even years. I know people who have stalled in the anger stage and refused to move forward. Their lives are full of sadness, and their downhearted attitude repels others. I know one friend who hasn't yet found the strength to move on, so this has become her way of life—mad and bitter.

Let's walk through the six stages as I share some of my personal experience with each.

DR. JAMES MOORE'S SIX STAGES OF GRIEF

1. **Numbness:** At this stage, shock and denial help buffer the loss. These feelings hit immediately upon learning of the accident or death, and they arrive as a form of protection, numbing us to details and letting us take in only as much as our minds can absorb. As I began to write this book, I could not remember the name of the hospital in Knoxville where Morgan was taken after the accident. I also forgot the name of an intern who was there that night, even though she was from our hometown and was a distant relative. My mind held no memory of who she was. None. Some details remain very clear, while others I can't recollect

at all. Perhaps God gives us only what we can manage during a traumatic situation and leaves the rest on the cutting-room floor.

2. Anger: Emotions run high in this stage, and when grief feels unbearable, we often look for someone to blame. In our case, a third party was responsible for the hit-and-run accident that killed our daughter. But even when there is no clear person at fault, a grieving parent may blame a spouse or even themselves. Anger at doctors who didn't heal, at God for letting this happen, even at the loved one who died for the decisions they made that may have led to their death, such as an overdose or suicide. Anger often acts as a way for the mind to make sense of the senseless. A child's death is too big a burden to bear, and when there is nowhere for that pain to go, it can spill over onto the people closest to us or lead to self-destructive behaviors. I've learned to accept that there are some things we simply cannot control, and placing blame on others does no good in the end. This stage is a vital part of the healing process. It provides a temporary structure to the chaos of early grief. It allows you to discharge the intense emotional pressure that comes with a sudden void in your life.

3. Loneliness: Grief can lead to depression, anxiety, isolation, sleeplessness, and intense sadness. The normal routine of life has been dramatically turned upside down, and nothing can fill the hole where your loved one used to be. Loneliness can feel unbearable, which is why I found it so helpful to surround myself with friends and loved ones, even when a part of me wanted to isolate and grieve alone.

4. Questioning: The "what if" stage can be maddening, as we ask why this tragedy had to happen. This questioning phase gives us time to adjust to the reality of the situation and to accept that, sometimes, life has no reasonable answers. Eventually, we have to surrender our need to rationalize an irrational situation, accepting that even in the best circumstances, death makes no sense.

5. Guilt: This is when we ask, "Could I have done anything to prevent this?" Assuming we could have done something to prevent this loss leaves us shouldering the burden of death. In truth, we have little (if any) control over life events, so we cannot allow guilt to drown us. Eventually, we must find a way to let go of self-blame. It doesn't serve us in any healthy way.

6. Return to reality: Here is where we find acceptance and hope. This does not mean we are okay with the loss. We may still feel waves of numbness, anger, loneliness, questioning, or guilt. But in time, we can come to terms with the loss and develop a yearning to help others who face similar situations.

GRIEF BRINGS A WHIRLWIND OF EMOTIONS, sometimes all at once. One day you may feel better, and the next you might feel like pieces of shattered glass, trying to put your life back together. Some people never move on to the last stage of acceptance. Time allows us to view life from different perspectives. It allows us to decide how we react to demanding situations.

I choose to grieve as my heart tells me to, and I am not on anyone else's timeline. The truth is, I can't escape my consequences, but I can control how I deal with them. I find peace knowing my faith will see me through.

God is our protection and our strength.
He always helps in times of trouble.
So we will not be afraid even if the earth shakes,
or the mountains fall into the sea.
—Psalm 46:1–2

17

PARENTING 101: THE MIDDLE-SCHOOL YEARS

Every day begins with a new sunrise.
—Unknown

Middle school. This is the time in life when we think we know it all—the time when we're figuring out how to navigate social situations, academic challenges, and raging emotions. It is also when we get a little too big for our britches, as we say in the South.

I remember my middle-school years like they were yesterday.

I was twelve years old, and my mother had made me a delicate lavender Easter dress. It was detailed down to tiny pearl buttons. Not particularly loving the color or the dress, I thought it was a little too frilly for me. As I was trying it on the night before, I didn't care for the scratchy collar around my neck.

"Mom, this dress is sticking me," I complained, yanking on the delicate dotted Swiss material.

"Careful, Pam. You might tear it."

But I was too uncomfortable to listen to Mother's warnings. Before I knew it, I had ripped a six-inch line from my collar to the middle of my dress. My whining stopped, and I froze, sucking in my breath. This was bad—really bad. I had never defied my mother so blatantly, and look what had happened as a result.

I knew I was in big trouble. But all I could think was, How would I be able to wear the dress tomorrow with a big, gaping hole in the front?

"Mother, I didn't mean to tear the dress. I don't know how it happened. Please forgive me. It just tore as I was trying to get it off my neck. It was making me itch."

I held my breath as she said, "Pam, just take off the dress and let me see what I can do with it."

By then, it was a mess, so I left the room. Still, as bad as I felt, at least I wouldn't have to wear the itchy dress with all my other new Easter finery.

As Mother brought the dress into the den, she looked at me and sighed in disappointment. "I'll have to stitch the front up by hand for tomorrow. It will look awful, but at this late date, there's no other option. I sure put a lot of work into that dress, and it was so pretty."

Mom was already exhausted, and daggers went through me. The dress really had been very pretty—until I'd ruined it.

Still, she didn't reprimand me, even though I'm sure I deserved a good one. I could stand a lot of scolding, but I couldn't stand letting my mother down. How would I ever make this up to her?

Instead of appreciating her hard work and devotion, my whining and stubbornness had ruined the dress.

When I went to bed, Mother was still repairing the dress and making it into something that would suffice for Easter. Embarrassed, I showed up that Sunday at church in the lovely lavender dress, with its six-inch stitched-up tear front and center.

Looking back, I think my mother knew exactly how to punish me. It was to make me wear the not-so-perfect dress for Easter Sunday.

No substitutes.

In her own gentle way, she was teaching me a lesson. And it was one I remembered.

We all have those growing-up moments, those core memories of choices we regret. I had mine, and Morgan did too. The lessons learned from our trials make us wiser and stronger.

As it turned out, the apple doesn't fall far from the tree. By not listening to my mother's warnings, I had torn that beautiful dress and learned my lesson. Like me, Morgan had a distressing moment when she found herself in hot water too.

As a young teen, Morgan's partner in crime was her friend Karen. Together, these sweet girls often landed in a bit of mischief. Usually, it was innocent enough, nothing that would leave lasting impact or cause any real harm. But one day, the girls came up with a brazen idea. Despite having no driver's license and still being too young to drive legally, Morgan decided to "steal" her brother's Jeep for a joyride.

Later, Morgan told me the whole story. Of course, she led the charge, and it was fun and exciting—until it went sideways.

"Kirk's not home," she explained to Karen. "We'll just drive down the street and back. My parents will be gone for a few hours. They'll never know."

"Let's go," Karen agreed, always eager to follow Morgan on any fun adventure.

At fourteen years of age, neither Morgan nor Karen had many driving lessons under their belt, but that didn't stop Morgan from grabbing the keys and taking the wheel as if she were an old pro. With giggly excitement, she backed the Jeep out of the driveway, bragging, "This isn't hard at all."

With Karen riding shotgun, the two daredevils made their way through the neighborhood, beaming with pride as if they'd just catapulted into adulthood. But as they reached the end of the street, it was time to turn around. That's when Morgan's limited driving skills became apparent.

Failing to navigate the U-turn, Morgan steered the Jeep off the pavement and into the mud. Not just a little mud, but mud so deep the wheels were spinning. Despite her best attempts, she could not steer the Jeep free. In fact, the harder she tried, the deeper the tires sank into the swampy earth.

"Hold on," Morgan warned her friend. Then she gunned the gas pedal, desperate to break the vehicle free of the muck.

Before the girls realized what was happening, they found themselves nearly upside down as the Jeep flipped over onto its side. Morgan yelled to Karen in a panic, "Are you all right?"

Thankfully, neither girl was injured, but they were shaken as they realized the trouble they'd caused. "What are we going to do?" Morgan shrieked, unbuckling the seat belt in a frantic rush.

"My door's jammed," Karen said, as Morgan came to the same realization on her side of the car.

"We're jammed in by the mud," Morgan wailed. "We'll have to climb out of the window."

After working themselves free of the sideways Jeep, the girls stood on the hot asphalt and stared at Kirk's prized possession, now an overturned mess at the end of the street. Morgan's heart hammered against her ribs as she tried to puzzle out a solution. The thrill of the crime and the rush of wind through her hair from only minutes earlier had vanished, replaced with guilt and shame.

With a sob catching in her throat, Morgan imagined Kirk's face, then her parents' faces. She would be grounded for life with no parole.

"Kirk will be furious," Morgan said, pacing up and down the side of the street. "And my parents!"

Not knowing what else to do, she walked to her grandfather's house at the other end of the street. Rushing through the door, she exclaimed, "Pop, I got Kirk's Jeep stuck in mud." Wringing her hands, she squealed through tears. "Help me get it back home, please!"

Of course, Pop came to the rescue and enlisted the help of another trusted neighbor. With the right tools at the ready, the two men managed to turn the Jeep upright.

"You're lucky you didn't damage Kirk's vehicle," Pop said calmly. "No dents, no parts falling off. Not a scratch on it. Only mud on a white Jeep."

But mud was everywhere—inside and out.

Both girls watched as Pop drove the Jeep home and parked it in the driveway. "You two better get busy washing every inch of this Jeep until it shines," he said sternly. "And let this be a lesson never to venture out like this again."

"Never again, Pop. I promise," Morgan announced. "Thank you so much for helping. Kirk would've killed me if he'd seen his Jeep like that. You can't tell anyone. Please?"

"It'll be our secret," Pop assured her, promising the neighbor wouldn't tell either.

"Oh, Pop! You seriously just saved my life!"

After scrubbing her brother's prized vehicle, Morgan carefully drove it back into the garage, leaving no sign of the afternoon ordeal.

It was two years before I learned of this deep, dark family secret. Morgan had waited until Kirk was away at college to tell us the story. Even though he was away from home, she still felt the sting of his anger over the phone after she confessed.

Horrified by her deception, I gave Morgan a good scolding. Then I questioned my dad about his help with the cover-up.

Pop laughed. "There was no need to tell you, Pam. Morgan was so scared and full of remorse. She had learned her lesson."

We all have those growing-up moments—decisions we regret, mistakes we make, choices that lead us the wrong direction. I certainly had mine, and Morgan had hers. But the lessons we learn from those trials can make us wiser and stronger.

Morgan never took her brother's Jeep again, and she learned that when she found herself in trouble, she had loved ones who would help her find her way through it.

Our local elementary school offered an enrichment class for bright students. The class met twice a week and involved the kids in fun, high-interest topics. Morgan had tested into the program and enjoyed being pulled from the regular classroom with her friends.

In fourth grade, she tested into the official "gifted" class, another pullout program for advanced students. All through elementary school, she enjoyed being involved and participated with enthusiasm. But as she transitioned to sixth grade, her attitude changed.

"I'm not going to the gifted program this year," she proclaimed the day before school started.

"Of course you are," I explained, assuming she was confused about her schedule.

"No, I'm not. Most of my friends won't be in there, and I'll be with people I don't know," she argued.

Surprised at the sudden shift in attitude, I tried to reason with her. "Morgan, I don't think it will matter if your friends are in the class or not. This is an opportunity for you to have challenging activities. It should be fun."

"No way! I don't want to be in a smart class. Just let me stay in the regular classroom," she ranted as she tossed her ponytail and crossed her arms. The middle-school attitude was showing.

This shocked me because it was a complete turnaround. She had always loved the gifted class. Now I realized, it was all about her peers, and they were taking a more important role in her life.

Her decision rang a bell because I had just finished my certification for teaching gifted students, and I'd studied this very issue, which often affects girls—especially *middle-school girls.*

And here we were living the very problem I had studied in my college classes.

Research by gifted specialists suggested that by middle school, girls tend to lose interest and drop out of gifted education classes. At that age, social pressure takes precedence, and being different from the mainstream peer group can be too much. Blending in with the crowd becomes the priority.

I had just studied this research, but never in a million years did I think it would happen to my daughter. Morgan had always had a mind of her own. Strong-willed, independent, and spunky, she was a true leader by nature, not the kind of girl to shrink herself in the name of conformity.

This conversation went round and round until I finally turned to her gifted teacher, Mrs. Linda, and told her about the changes in Morgan's attitude.

"What can I do?" I asked. "Many students would love to be in this program, and she's just going to throw away this opportunity?"

Patiently, Mrs. Linda said, "Just have her come for the first week.

Some of her friends will be there, and we'll have fun units this fall. I think she'll like them."

With this compromise, Morgan reluctantly agreed to attend the gifted class. Imagine my relief when she came home saying, "This semester we're studying the stock market and researching stocks. Mrs. Linda will give everyone the same amount of pretend money to buy and trade. At the end of the game in December, the student team that's made the most money will win a limo ride to lunch with the teacher. I hope my team wins."

She eased into sixth grade with all the new experiences and seemed to enjoy taking part in the gifted class. Several of her friends were in the class, and the intellectual challenge kept her interested.

When December came, Morgan jumped in the car after school, bursting with excitement. With shining eyes, she told me, "We won! Our team won the stock market game, and we'll go to lunch in a limo during school. Isn't that the coolest thing ever?"

"I'm so proud of you!" I beamed with pride. "You worked so hard looking at stock prices every day. It paid off."

And just like that, she was learning new things again, all because of a creative teacher who not only got her attention but also kept her engaged by making learning fun.

Morgan was hooked from then on. She had no complaints about being pulled from the mainstream classroom, and she enjoyed the sixth, seventh, and eighth-grade gifted classes with enthusiasm.

I was glad Morgan was able to overcome the pressure that causes some girls to pull back from gifted programs. As a career educator, I was not going to let my daughter fall into underachievement. That was one statistic I was glad to help break.

Research states that middle-school girls need the support of their parents and teachers to resist peer and societal pressures. Without close parental and teacher guidance, girls may hold back from reaching their full potential.

The middle-school years can be challenging for parents and students alike. But the decisions we make at that stage can guide teens through those tumultuous years with love and kindness. Just as my mother had not made a big fuss when I'd ripped my Easter dress as a girl, I tried to navigate my children's middle-school years by offering grace when they made mistakes. Like Mother had modeled for me, I wanted to help them learn valuable lessons without sending them into a rebellious cycle of shame and dishonesty.

As adolescents navigate this tumultuous stage of life, their growing autonomy often results in flawed judgment. Mistakes can become an essential aspect of their growth and development. Taking Kirk's Jeep proved to be a nightmare trip and a hard lesson for Morgan. She was sure she did not want to be in the gifted class, but she was happy to take part in the end. Her peers were important, and she wanted to be with them in class, but she also enjoyed the friendships she made in the advanced class.

Just as Morgan learned that she could benefit from taking the gifted classes, I learned that, as a parent, I needed to give clear signals that were easy to follow while also allowing middle schoolers to develop a sense of agency in their decision-making. Nurturing them requires a balance between providing guidance and allowing children to learn from their experiences.

While we can't always make decisions for our children or shield them from every hardship, it's important to acknowledge that both children and parents will make mistakes. Kids as well as parents need forgiveness and grace at every stage of life.

As parents, we will continue to care for and be concerned about our children as long as they live. It's in moments of uncertainty that families find ways to support each other through mistakes and triumphs alike. The ultimate path through adolescence is not about perfection but about learning to navigate the challenges together, with understanding and love at the core.

18

TRIGGERS

Keep your face to the sunshine and you cannot see the shadows.
—Helen Keller

I know parents, like me, who have lost a child, and we agree that the shock never goes away. All these years after Morgan's death, I still face trigger moments that are hard to deal with. At first, I had a hard time with music, especially in church. I think I cried during every service for the first year.

Certain things bring back such strong memories. It takes only the sweet fragrance of her favorite perfume or a verse of a song to bring me to my knees.

In his book *For One More Day,* Mitch Albom wrote, "When someone is in your heart, they are never truly gone. They can come back to you even at unlikely times."

Over and over, ordinary things can throw us back into remembrance, bringing a wave of grief, usually followed by a torrent of tears.

One of the first public places I went to, other than Kroger, was my spin class at the YMCA, just around the corner from my home. It felt like a safe way to begin after a month of being home alone in my grief. I needed to get out of the house, and my gym friends felt like family.

The class members welcomed me back with open arms. "We're glad you're here with us today. We've been thinking of you and missing you," said our instructor, Meg.

"I feel the same way. Glad to be back," I said with a smile.

But as class began, the warm-up song was "I Hope You Dance" by Lee Ann Womack. I froze and immediately teared up. It was a song from Morgan's memorial service, and I had not heard it since then.

I told the woman next to me, and the instructor quickly changed the song.

Out of the blue, a song can snap us right back to a painful moment in time. I still have a hard time hearing that song today, but I love how it embraces Morgan's spirit and love of dance.

I will say that the trigger moments have lessened as the years have gone by, but they still surface when I least expect them. Sixteen years had passed since Morgan died when another trigger hit me hard.

It happened when I was in the shower. I looked up and saw my hair wrap, the one I used to put my wet hair up after washing. But it had turned into a faded, limp towel that barely had a loop left. It was worn and needed to be replaced. Since they came in packages of two, I thought, "That's good. I'll have one for Morgan to use."

Suddenly, I started crying, really sobbing, at the thought that I would never get to share the hair wrap—or anything—with her ever again. That hole in my heart widened with every breath. It was just a worn-out piece of cloth, but it reminded me that my daughter was gone. The trigger hit me hard, and it came out of nowhere.

Another time, during one of my first grocery store visits, it was a beautiful day, and I was feeling fine until I passed the aisle where the Milano cookies were stocked. Suddenly, a complete sadness hit me because Milano cookies were her favorite sweet treat. I stood there, tears falling, as I stared at the cookies. I wondered why Morgan couldn't still be here, sharing in the simple pleasures of life. The happy day came crashing down as the realization of everything I had lost hit me again. I absentmindedly picked up a package and put it in the shopping cart. Perhaps going home with the cookies would make me feel close to her again, just by holding something she loved. Someone passed me, picked up the cookies, and moved on.

I remembered when Milano cookies were just cookies.

I yearned for the time when a cookie did not have the ability to take my breath away.

Triggers.

We have no warning.

Whether we are out in a group in public or in the privacy of our own shower at home, they can strike with a vengeance. I guess I'm destined to have these moments for the rest of my life. This is yet another aspect of my "new normal."

19

UNRAVELING THE HOLIDAYS

Stormy or sunny days, glorious or lonely nights, I maintain an attitude of gratitude.
—Maya Angelou

Holidays can be the most dreadful times, especially during the first few years after losing a loved one. Intense anxiety can build up as those sentimental seasons draw near and a chair sits empty.

"We're skipping Christmas," I announced to Mike as our first Christmas without Morgan approached. "I don't even want to hear holiday music. Those songs only remind me of the happiness I no longer have in my heart."

The stark contrast between glowing Christmas lights and the darkness of our sorrow can be difficult to manage. I could not possibly face decorating the tree. "So many memories are attached to Christmas," I said to Mike. "I can't face the heartache. I can't decorate this year."

"I agree," he said, supporting me in his steady way. "We'll leave all the decorations in the attic. It would be too hard to look at them with Morgan gone."

Our enormous Christmas tree held many of Morgan's and Kirk's handmade ornaments from their elementary years—the little green trees from the Christmas tree farm, with their pictures at the top like gold stars; the handprint Christmas tree with their large elementary-school signatures on the back; and all the framed pictures from visits with Santa. We also had memorable souvenirs from vacations—skiing ornaments adorned with the place and date; pictures from school trips to Washington, DC, the Statue of Liberty ornament, and Morgan's bright-red, Saks shopping bag.

All these treasures triggered memories of the wonderful times we'd shared as a family, but at this early stage, I could not begin to look at them. Each served as a reminder of what we had lost, causing a painful jolt to my system. All those sentimental treasures stood as proof that our daughter was gone and that we would never be able to celebrate Christmas with her again. We could no longer reminisce about snow-covered slopes or beach trips or field trips without being overcome by grief.

"Let's break with tradition. A trip to the beach will help," I told Mike and Kirk. "We all need a change of scenery."

So, on that first Christmas, only three months after we lost Morgan, we went to Destin, Florida, to stay at my good friend Kathy's beachfront condo. There, we could grieve on our own terms and avoid the usual Christmas traditions.

At the water's edge, my sorrow met a tranquil spot as I closed my eyes and let the memories come. Hours from home, I surrendered to the crashing waves. I let the cool sand soothe my toes as the rhythmic waves rippled over my bare feet. The vastness of the turquoise ocean reminded me that I was not alone. I felt the presence of our Creator, the giver of all life. My senses sharpened as the seagulls called and the waves ebbed and flowed. The briny taste on my lips reminded me of summers spent gliding through the surf on rafts. Such endless memories of the joy Morgan discovered when the rushing waves brought her ashore with laughter, only for her to swim back out for more.

What a feeling of carefree fun we'd shared at this very beach. The memories could have crushed me, but instead, I found inner peace here at the water's edge. No book, writer, or picture can capture the calm and serenity I felt, a sudden closeness to God. Yes, the water gave me a calmer view of my life, and even in raw stages of grief, I stood before the open sea, and I gave thanks.

The ocean's roar became music to my weary soul.

After this transformative moment, I returned to Kirk and Mike, who also seemed to feel more at peace in this beautiful setting. All was going well until we went to one of our favorite restaurants for dinner. After we arrived, we decided it was just too hard to stay. It had been Morgan's favorite restaurant too, and her presence was with us everywhere we went.

"I don't know what I was thinking," I confessed. "I thought if we could get away from home, we could run away from grief, but the heartache is still all around us."

On Christmas Eve, with no restaurants open, we opted for a frozen pizza from a drugstore. At that point, our meal was meaningless. We were not sitting together for a special family feast. We were merely existing in survival mode, trying to take one breath at a time through unbearable grief.

As time has gone by, I have not thrown out all our holiday traditions, but I have changed things. I get out some of the Christmas decorations, but I only set up the big tree if the grandchildren come into town. Paring down the holidays without giving everything up has been a great compromise.

As for Mother's Day and Father's Day, we must remain thankful for the children still with us and not forget them. I knew one friend who would not acknowledge her two grown children after her daughter died. She was missing countless joys with her grandchildren because she was locked so deep in mourning for her lost daughter. That was an extreme case, and I suggested she see a counselor, but all parents must find a way to survive those painful holiday seasons.

The first Thanksgiving was hard for our family because it was so close to Morgan's "date." In my mind, I had absolutely nothing to be thankful for, and it was a distressing day to get through. Now as the years pass, I try to surround myself with family and friends and think of all the good things I can be thankful for each year.

Healing is a gradual, tender process, not a sudden recovery. Each year, these significant dates may awaken the pain of absence, filling you with deep longing and sadness. Yet with each passing celebration, there's an opportunity to share cherished memories and acknowledge the love that remains. Over time, new traditions begin to form as we honor our loved ones, celebrate the happy memories, and bring joy to those who are still with us. Unexpected moments of happiness can happen, even amid the lingering ache.

WAYS TO HONOR YOUR LOVED ONE ON SPECIAL DAYS

1. Plant flowers at gravesites for beauty in every season.
2. Scatter a loved one's ashes in a place they loved.
3. Plant a tree in their memory.
4. Create a special social media post with memories.
5. Donate to a favorite charity or church in their honor.
6. Wear something meaningful—clothes, jewelry, or perfume —to remember your loved one. I was given a necklace with Morgan's name in Morse code. It is silver and special because Sherry, the mother of one of Morgan's friends and a member of our Grace for Grief group, gave it to me.
7. Make a memorial quilt. My sister Donna made one from the T-shirts we print each year for the charity golf tournaments we host in Morgan's memory. Morgan's sorority at UT also made a quilt from her sorority T-shirts.
8. Journal or write a letter to your child on this special day.
9. Light a sky lantern and release it at night. I had the joy of doing this on the beach in Destin with friends. It was a special thrill to see the lantern ascend over the water.
10. Start a memorial scholarship in your child's honor.
11. Create a memory garden. A dear friend of Mike's mother "Cousin Tuny" had a memory garden and honored us with a stone in Morgan's memory.
12. Make a memory box containing your favorite items from

your loved one: a piece of jewelry, a photo, a card, or a drawing.

13. Donate to or volunteer with a charity or a cause that was important to your loved one, such as an animal shelter or a soup kitchen.

Perhaps the American humorist and author Erma Bombeck said it best: "On Mother's Day, I can think of no mother more deserving than a mother who had to give one back."

Bless all mothers who have endured the pain of losing a child.

20

THE DATE

All of a sudden, my life is divided into before and after.
—Unknown

The anniversary of your child's death—your date—will be difficult. The grief will rise as the day approaches, and it will continue to be one of the most dreaded days of each year.

As the first anniversary approached, friends told me to prepare ahead of time by planning an activity that Morgan would have enjoyed. Some suggested I visit the cemetery to refresh her resting place with flowers or mementos.

I used that day to reflect in the stillness of nature around me.

Every year since, I've spent time alone on this difficult day. I give myself time to picture Morgan, imagining her at the age she'd be now. I ponder...what would she be doing? Would she be married? Would she have children of her own?

I grant myself permission and time to cry whenever the mood strikes me. While many people may tell you not to cry, and others may try to avoid tears, I believe they come for a reason. Tears can nourish us as we move through grief. I don't deny myself the opportunity to cry or even try to hide it. For me, crying releases the heavy feelings and gripping anxiety that build up within me. Tears free us from continuing tension.

Maybe that's why Jesus wept after Lazarus died. He understood the power of tears, and he shares our tears today.

He gets us. He knows the hurt is deep. I encourage you to express your emotions in healthy ways. Release the anger, hurt, loneliness, or sadness with tears, if you are able.

Jesus set the example. He gave us permission to cry.

The death of a loved one has far-reaching effects on everyone involved, including close friends. Robyn, a dear friend of Morgan, posted these words on the seventh anniversary of our daughter's passing.

> What a hard day today is. Today, seven years ago, so many of us lost the greatest of friends, we lost the closest confidante, lost a part of ourselves. Morgan will live on in our hearts forever, and I know so many will cherish the memories we had with her. I count myself lucky to have had her as a friend, and just a suggestion, be a little more Morgan today. Be a little more kind, more loving, more southern, and a little more fun to everyone today. She is so missed. The impact she left will never be forgotten.

Wow! Be a little more Morgan.

BIRTHDAYS WERE CELEBRATED BIG in the McCarty household. Morgan was born on December 16, which fell too close to all the Christmas events, so each year, we celebrated her birthday in October instead, hosting hayrides and bonfires as an annual tradition.

The first year after we lost Morgan, I knew those months were going to be especially painful. Between birthdays and holidays, we were walking through a field of emotional landmines. Still, I didn't want her birthday to go by without doing something special. So, as difficult as I knew it would be, I invited some of her friends to honor what would have been Morgan's twenty-first birthday.

Nothing gives me more joy than being around the friends she loved so much. While it was not easy to celebrate Morgan's life in those first few months after she died, we did cut a birthday cake and share special memories. One of her friends, Kara, shared, "Morgan would love us all getting together tonight, and she would especially love the chocolate cake," and everyone agreed.

Now, we celebrate Morgan's birthday every year. It can be as simple as having her favorite meal or going to one of her favorite restaurants, but we don't let the occasion go by without special notice.

Recently, I talked with my Grace for Grief group about ways we can celebrate the birthdays of our children. Some like to spend the day giving to a cause or a group that was connected to their loved one. Some take food to the local soup kitchen, others volunteer with a grade school class, and others invite friends and family to a special birthday meal. There are so many ways to honor your loved one, helping transform your pain into a positive action.

One year, I decided to go to the local bakery and pay for someone's birthday cake on the day of Morgan's birth (December 16). The two stipulations were: I was to remain anonymous, and it needed to be a child's birthday cake. I wrote the following note and left it with the cake.

> Dear Mom,
>
> Today is my daughter's 25th birthday and the 4th one in heaven.
>
> In memory of her, I paid for your child's cake.
> Please enjoy and make wonderful memories.
> Hug your child tight and cherish your days.
> You never know if this will be your last one.
> Love,
> A grieving Mom

As I was paying for the cake, one of the clerks said, "I know you. You are Morgan McCarty's mother. I went to school with her."

A familiar panic began to grow in my stomach as I realized my identity was blown.

Standing there in my gym clothes, I had nowhere to hide, so I told her, "Yes," and she said, "Can you show the others her picture?"

As I got out her picture for the others in the store, the floodgates opened. I not only started crying, but sobbing. Soon, I had the entire baking staff crying too. The employees came from behind the counter, and we all hugged and shed tears together. As they passed her picture around, they wanted to know more about her.

Through my tears, I explained, "Morgan died from a hit-and-run accident at UT when she was a junior in college. That happened in 2006, and we miss her every day."

The girl who knew her said, "I was younger than Morgan, but I knew her from school. She was a cheerleader. I remember her smile and how nice she was to me as a younger student."

I had hoped to go into the bakery, make the donation, and make a quick exit. I certainly didn't expect to break down in the shop. But that's how grief works. Triggers can happen when we least expect them. That day, pulling Morgan's photo from my purse became the trigger.

It was already an emotional day, and it didn't take much to snowball me into a crying mess. Sometimes the smallest moment can throw off the normal rhythm of an entire day. We certainly don't plan for it to happen, but as I left the shop, I was grateful the girl behind the counter had remembered Morgan's kind spirit. I was thankful the staff had surrounded me with love as we all acknowledged the light my daughter had brought to this world. What could have caused me to flee in embarrassment, with tears streaming down my cheeks, turned into a beautiful moment of connection and a special chance to honor my beloved daughter.

Another of Morgan's good friends, Rachael, posted this on the fifth birthday after Morgan was gone.

> Tonight, I raise my glass to a toast. To the most charming and beautiful woman who has ever graced me with her presence. A beauty that made men stop in their tracks. Who taught me to love without holding back, trust without reservation, and live each day to its fullest, no regrets. Your spirit, enthusiasm, spunk, and complete love for life lives on in every person you touched. Carpe Diem, my friend, and Happy Birthday to my favorite Princess.

We all love and miss you very much. Cheers!

The first birthday after Morgan's death, a close teacher friend acknowledged the difficult day by gifting me a special devotion book, *The Daily Light*. Mrs. Angela was a powerhouse of faith who would spend her lunch breaks by herself, praying for others. What a role model she was to all the younger teachers.

She explained, "I've had this book for a while, but the Lord impressed upon my heart to wait and give it to you today, on Morgan's birthday. Hopefully, it will bless you as it has blessed me and others. Daily, as I read from it, I pray for those to whom it has been given."

What a blessing that she had waited all those months before giving it to me. If she had given it to me right after Morgan was killed, when my brain was still in a fog, I wouldn't have been able to read or comprehend any of it. She'd found the perfect timing and a meaningful way to honor Morgan's birthday.

Just as she'd hoped, reading the devotions brought me great comfort. The verse selected for December 16 (Morgan's birthday) spoke specifically to my needs on that day.

"The mountains may disappear,
and the hills may come to an end,
but my love will never disappear;
my promise of peace will not come to an end,"
says the Lord who shows mercy to you.
—Isaiah 54:10

21

THE HARD GOODBYE

I couldn't see how the sun would shine in the midst of darkness. Sorrow, however, turns out to be not a state but a process.
—C. S. Lewis

The moment a child leaves us, a parent's heart feels different. Medically, this condition is now called "broken heart syndrome," but grieving parents knew this long before it was diagnosed and named by doctors.

The pain of losing a child is emotional and spiritual, but it's also physical. It can feel as intense as having a part of your body traumatically severed. Unlike most wounds, this soul-deep ache never goes away. That broken heart is so heavy, and in many cases, the more time you've spent with a loved one, the more intensely you feel the impact of your loss.

We were in physical and mental pain when we arrived home from the hospital and began planning Morgan's funeral. Friends had already come to our house, preparing food, mowing the yard, doing everything they could think of to help us since we had been in Knoxville for five days.

Family began to fly in from out of state, and it was comforting to have loved ones around us, even though it was hard to process what was happening.

I felt overwhelmed and exhausted. Choosing clothes, taking a shower, and even brushing my teeth all seemed to take more energy than I had. Friends guided us when to get up in the morning, when to eat, and when to go to the funeral home. We were just going through the motions, too numb to think logically for ourselves.

Obituaries were written and sent to the papers. Our minister from First United Methodist Church came to our home to go over his plans for the service.

Our good friend David was asked to sing two songs that Morgan loved: "I Can Only Imagine" and "I Hope You Dance." He stripped them down to solo guitar and voice, offering an intimate and honorable memorial to our daughter.

My friend Teresa, who had known Morgan since she was a little girl, gave a personal and heartfelt tribute that gave everyone a glowing look into her short life. A choir was chosen. So many important decisions were made in a haze because my brain couldn't understand or process anything.

The big question everyone kept asking me was: when would the funeral be held?

Thursday would have been the logical day, but that Thursday was September 28—my birthday. I couldn't bear the thought of burying my daughter on the day I was supposed to celebrate my own life. We chose Friday, September 29, instead. That date also allowed more UT students to travel from Knoxville, including Morgan's sorority sisters, who planned to sing at the service.

Our minister, Dr. Paul Clayton, had known Morgan since she was eight years old. He had watched her grow up and ministered to her at every step of her life. During her funeral service, he shared that over a thousand loved ones had crowded into the sanctuary to honor Morgan. Then he said:

To use an older expression, Morgan took life by the lapels! So many have witnessed that reality with expressions like: Life lived to the fullest with abandonment. Lived with risk and vulnerability. Tossed caution to the wind. Lived without fear. Lived like life was going out of style. And as Mike would say, she would slide in sideways.

> Myriad images will flood your minds and hearts for years to come. Hold on to the memory of students and officials and the medical teams assembled at the hospital in Knoxville, flowers at the intersection of 17th and Highland Avenue. Keep before your minds the images of marches to the scene, the campus candlelight vigils with scriptures, prayers, singing "Amazing Grace," and personal tributes. Behold a sea of blue ribbons and pink bracelets. Fill your heart with the flood of responses on Morgan's Facebook page. You will long remember the caring Kappa Kappa Gamma memorial with irises, lanterns, and blue ribbons, and most of all their faithful presence. And maybe most of all, hold on to this moment. Here are gathered a thousand of Morgan's best friends and yours. Some have traveled far, so devoted, loyal, warm, generous, loving, and caring, to this place where we celebrate Morgan's life in the context of her faith and ours, in the presence of the living, loving, Eternal God!

I couldn't stop my tears as he offered us such healing words. Around me, many dabbed their eyes. I grabbed Kirk's hand.

> Here in Jackson, you are surrounded and supported by loving family and dear friends, this First Church, and this whole community. Friends—never stronger or more present—embracing each other in the face of the mystery and fragility of life itself. Life is held by a thread; one drop of water, one breath of air can kill us. Hold on to God and claim our interdependence with each other and our utter dependence on HIM.
>
> Morgan majored in life. At UT she may have been majoring in communications, but she was already majoring in life. A lesson to learn from Morgan's life might be that we give up any half-heartedness about life and all its relationships and instead

> live every day to the fullest! She lived only twenty years, but she packed so much life into those years!
>
> As some of you gathered in Knoxville, you sang, 'Amazing Grace,' which ends with: 'When we've been there…ten thousand years, bright shining as the sun, We've no less days to sing God's praise than when we first begun!'
>
> Let me rephrase. The end of all that has been, the edge of all that is yet to be. Whisper it or shout it. Just hold on to the truth of life and faith.

Paul closed the service with two songs we'd found on Morgan's iPod that we, as family, had requested: "Shout to the Lord" and "The Hallelujah Chorus," a joyous crescendo of triumph and faith, hope and love. It ends with: "He shall reign forever and ever and ever and ever and ever. AMEN!"

MY DAD WAS TOLD that Morgan's visitation was the largest that the funeral home had ever hosted. Though we were not aware at the time that hundreds and hundreds of friends were lining up outside the door and around the block, tears of sympathy flowed as Mike, Kirk, and I thanked each person who came to support us that night.

As much as I tried to remain in the present, the entire evening was a nightmarish blur, with my raw emotions on edge. I do remember asking everyone we talked to that night to pray for our family, and prayers definitely held us up through the funeral service that night and the following day.

ABOUT HALFWAY THROUGH THE VISITATION, our friend and attorney, Alan, pulled us to the side and told us, "We just got a call from the Knoxville Police Department. They've caught the man responsible for Morgan's accident. He's in jail."

This news gave us a sense of relief, knowing the man was off the streets and couldn't take another life. But at the same time, it gave us little satisfaction because it couldn't bring Morgan back to us.

As Terri Irwin so eloquently stated after losing her husband, Steve, "Grief is never something you get over. You don't wake up one morning and say, 'I've conquered that; now I'm moving on.' It's something that walks beside you every day. And if you can learn how to manage it and honor the person that you miss, you can take something that is incredibly sad and have some form of positivity."

This state of grief was something I now understood. It's something that walks with you every day. Would there ever be sunny days again? There were many moments when I struggled to go on. But like Terri Irwin, I did see the sun rise again.

And you will too.

Sorrow has its ugly moments, but despite the despair, we can choose to face another day. We simply have to set our sights on the sun and not on the darkness.

As hard as it is, you do have one thing going for you. God is with you in the tough times and never leaves you.

There will never be night again. They will not need the light of a lamp or the light of the sun, because the Lord God will give them light. And they will rule as kings forever and ever.
—Revelation 22:5

One of the hardest things to experience was seeing our child's name carved on the headstone with the dates listed. It was shocking. Somehow, even after all we had been through, this made her death final. The words said it all for us.

Morgan Leah McCarty
December 16, 1985–September 23, 2006
"Our Princess"

Someone once said to me, "Pam, I don't know how you do it."

I said simply, "I wasn't given a choice."

Life will hurt all of us in one way or another, some to greater degrees than others, and there will never be a reason good enough to justify the suffering and cruelty we endure. But I want you to know that you *can* endure it, even if you aren't fortunate enough to be surrounded by community, family, or friends to support you through the storm.

If you're feeling alone in your despair and grief, I want you to know you are not alone. You have an entire community of bereaved parents who understand your journey and are walking with you, step-by-step. And you have God. He promises never to leave us, especially during our darkest hours.

Whether you are someone with a firm faith foundation or someone who has never really learned spiritual practices, I encourage you to rely on that greater source of strength. Faith will carry you when you're feeling too much pain to keep breathing. It will get you through to the next sunrise, one breath at a time. It will anchor you in love and light and remind you that you are still here for a reason, and you can still choose to love and be loved. Even when facing such immeasurable grief and pain, you are still loved.

22

TEN MINUTES AT A TIME

Tears are the silent language of grief.
—Voltaire

The loneliest time after a tragedy is the week or month when everyone goes home, and your new normal begins. The silence feels deafening when the crowds disappear, and you are left with a gaping hole in your heart.

For me, nighttime is the hardest time of the day. Night feels lonelier and never-ending.

After three days of tossing and turning, I finally fell asleep from pure exhaustion. I wondered if this was how I would feel for the rest of my life. I was not the same person I had been before, and I knew I'd never be that person again. I tried not to let my mind wander too far into the future because it was too much to process. I couldn't imagine my life without Morgan. All I saw was loss.

So, I learned to take each day ten minutes at a time. That was the threshold for me. Ten minutes. What do I need to do right now, within the next ten minutes? Beyond that, everything was a blur.

Day by day, life started to return to "normal" for everyone else. Kirk returned to Nashville for work. Out-of-town relatives flew home, and my husband went back to his job. I found myself home alone during the day, and I had a hard time even getting dressed each morning. Simple, mundane tasks were so hard to get through. One of my favorite escapes had always been reading, but I could no longer manage more than a few brief paragraphs because I had so much difficulty concentrating. I couldn't imagine tackling the stack of thank-you notes that spilled over the dining room table. My appetite changed. I didn't want to eat, let alone cook anything. I would walk by a photograph of Morgan and burst into tears—not pretty tears, but big, ugly sobs.

Looking at her beautiful picture was just too painful, so I put away all the photos of Morgan, tucking them out of sight.

No matter how hard I tried to move forward, the same thoughts kept running through my head.

She's not going to call to tell me about her classes.

I won't get an update on her social life or hear about her next social mixer.

There will be no panicky rush to find the perfect costume for the latest themed dance.

The phone will be silent instead of ringing several times each day with her peppy updates.

Even our Sheltie dog, Mack, sat solemnly at the front door, waiting for her return.

What about the rest of her clothes? For some people, it takes a long time before they're able to sort through their loved one's things. Sometimes it takes years. Others do it quickly or store the items out of sight in boxes for later. Some donate clothes to charity, and still others make treasures out of their loved one's favorite belongings, like blankets or quilts or framed collages. I guess I did a little of all of that.

I had left many of Morgan's clothes and shoes at her apartment in Knoxville for her roommates to keep. One girl later told me she couldn't afford designer jeans, so she was thrilled to have a pair of Morgan's.

I remember when we bought them. Morgan had implored, "Since I'm so tall, this is the only brand that is long enough to fit me."

I'd bought right into her story. I knew she was weaseling me into buying an expensive pair of jeans, but she was right. It really had been hard to fit her long legs, so I agreed.

The things in her bedroom were left untouched until a flood four years later damaged her basement room. The water damage finally forced me to sort through her belongings.

I donated a lot of her clothes to charity, along with the bedding and curtains. They were still in good shape, and someone else could enjoy using them. I saved many of her special dresses because it was too hard to part with them, and perhaps, they could be saved for granddaughters someday.

Morgan's sorority at UT had a blanket made from all the sorority party shirts from her years at school. What a treasure! It means so much to have the last years of her life remembered in such a heartfelt way. My sister Donna made a quilt out of the T-shirts from our golf and dance fundraisers for the scholarship fund. Today, those two quilts are my favorites to cozy up with. It feels like wrapping myself in her arms.

There is no right or wrong way to handle a loved one's personal items. I thought of Morgan and smiled each time I sent something of hers to someone, hoping they would delight in them. I knew Morgan would want me to share her treasures with her beloved friends. With each donation, I pictured Morgan smiling with approval.

When grief gripped me in the aftermath of the tragedy, I became captive to my own destructive thoughts. But as time passed, I gradually put her pictures on display again, and it became a little easier to see Morgan's beautiful face.

Losing a child is a unique kind of grief. The natural order of life is interrupted, and nothing about it feels acceptable, rational, or fair.

I have grieved the loss of parents, grandparents, uncles, and aunts—all of whom I loved dearly—but losing a child is unfathomable. It cannot be compared to any other death.

For a mother, a part of you is gone.

I had carried Morgan in my womb and brought her into this world. I was not supposed to outlive her. She and Kirk were supposed to stand together, united in life, supporting one another when they buried their parents someday.

But now I had to navigate not only the loss of what we'd had, but also the loss of all the hopes and dreams and promises of the future. The life I'd always envisioned for our family had been taken from all of us in an instant, and there was no easy way to find joy on the other side of such tremendous loss.

After my husband went back to work, I was alone at home and overwhelmed by all the flowers, sympathy cards, and gifts we had received, but I kept putting off sending thank-you notes. I still had plants in every room, even though I had given many to family and friends. We'd even received cards from kind strangers who had read about Morgan in the Knoxville and Memphis newspapers. Most shared their own experiences of losing someone close to them, offering thoughtful words of support and empathy.

When I opened the mail, I was amazed that so many people had taken the time to send a card or a book and share words of comfort and encouragement.

One of the most poignant items we received was from a lady I did not know. She lived in Knoxville, and she'd sent the letter to the sorority after reading the news report in *The Tennessean*. Her note was forwarded to us, postmarked September 26. In tiny, arthritic script, her message read:

> Dear Parents,
>
> My sincere sympathy to you in the tragic accidental death of Morgan. May God comfort you, and I pray the enclosed material will be a source of help and strength to you.
>
> In His Love,
> An 88-year-old Christian lady

In the envelope were four pamphlets on grief as well as a lovely poem she had written called "God's Loan." Her words shook me to my core, knowing that an elderly lady had seen the report and felt moved to reach out even though she did not know us. She shared such a meaningful act of Christian kindness and sympathy. After shedding tears of thanksgiving for such a gracious woman, I wanted to respond and give personal thanks for her kind words, but with no return address, she remained anonymous. Just another act of God's love given to our household.

I could feel God's grace being poured out through all these people.

We had been carried through those first few weeks by prayer. God's presence was so real as we faced Morgan's death and laid her to rest. I worried about how I would ever respond to all the acts of sympathy and kindness, but I did not want to send an impersonal card from the funeral home. Instead, I thought everyone deserved a personal thank-you from Mike and me. So, I called a few of my teacher friends, and within a few days, I had a small team of volunteers to help me.

We cleared off the dining room table, and we all wrote notes using samples I had already prepared. After a few days, all the cards were written and mailed. My group of friends saved me from drowning. Even though it took more time and effort, I believed I needed to express our gratitude with a personal response. It was as if this were one of the last acts I could do to honor Morgan's memory, but I would soon find out there were more ways to come.

They tried to heal my people's serious injuries
as if they were small wounds.
They said, "It's all right, it's all right."
But really, it is not all right.
—Jeremiah 6:14

23

MY LIFE PRESERVERS

Friends are like sunshine on a cloudy day.
—Unknown

As long as I live, I will never forget my family and friends who got me through the first dark days of grief. They kept my head above water.

Even after my out-of-town family had to return home, my friends in Jackson consoled me, wept with me, flooded me with cards, calls, and flowers, and stood by me. They were like family and truly saved our lives.

My sister-in-law, Denise, called me every day for almost a year. I looked forward to those chats, which were a daily act of loving comfort. Many church friends called and asked, "What do you need? How are you feeling?"

At that point, I honestly didn't know what I needed except prayers to get through the day.

A special friend announced one morning, "I'm coming by the house." Looking forward to the company, I was grateful she would help fill my empty day.

Another close friend, Molly, showed up with an armload of what she called "grief groceries." She did not ask what I needed, but what she brought certainly fit the bill—rotisserie chicken, sliced vegetables, peach ice cream, pizza, cookies, and plenty of Diet Coke. We enjoyed our favorite comfort foods without having to cook. Molly acted on instinct, and those groceries were an act of kindness for Mike and me. It's a good friend who knows what to bring without asking.

Friends also gave us gift cards to local restaurants. Those gifts allowed us to pick up fresh meals without having to go inside and see people. At that point, I was wearing my grief on my face and wasn't ready to interact in public.

Another church friend, Bill, showed up one day with what he called a "grief sundae."

"I didn't know what you needed," he said. "But I felt like this might help."

Indeed, it did! What a precious act of generosity to help brighten my day.

Another day, I was feeling overwhelmed by all the vases and pots of flowers from Morgan's memorial service. The doorbell rang, and I answered to find a church friend standing there with a watering can. Cathy explained, "All I could think about was all the flowers that you had to water."

"This is just what I needed," I said, thanking her for the thoughtful gesture. "It'll help me water all these plants."

What a blessing she gave me just by meeting my needs that day.

Grief groceries, a chocolate sundae, a watering can—all simple things that mean so much when your life is turned upside down. It almost seemed as if the moment I thought of a problem, exactly what I needed somehow found its way to my door. Each thoughtful offering filled a void in my day and made me smile. How lucky, I thought, to be surrounded by God's grace delivered through such caring friends. God really does meet our needs when we don't even know what they are. Even when I was too exhausted to pray, he never left me.

PEOPLE SOMETIMES ASSUME that after a few weeks or a month, we should be further along in our grief. In the fall of 2006, I was teaching gifted students and traveling to two schools across our district to work with students from kindergarten to fifth grade. My job was delightful, and I enjoyed helping students tackle new challenges.

But even a few weeks after losing Morgan, I was not in any shape to go back to teaching. So, I decided to take several months off.

I even entertained thoughts of early retirement, figuring I was so wounded I should never go back into the classroom. But as it turned out, that classroom became my salvation.

My husband had already returned to work in his quiet office, leaving me home by myself. Friends and family members were checking on me, but after a month or so of sitting home alone, I knew for sanity's sake that I needed to occupy my mind with something other than grief. The classroom was where I needed to be.

So, with apprehension and prayer, I returned to my job as a gifted teacher after six months off.

I rotated between two schools, and those teachers became my life preservers, welcoming me back with open arms. They supported me and, at the same time, gave me space.

Each day I returned to school to find a "happy" on my desk. That is what we call a small gift in the South. Every morning, the teachers in my hall left these little offerings, along with kind notes of encouragement and support to help get me through the day. Throughout the school year, I received candles, hand lotions, notepads, Diet Cokes, and just about every other little gift you could think of! The warmth and support from my colleagues uplifted me, and they never had to say a word.

I felt so loved and supported. I shudder to think that I almost did not return to school. Little did I know that my teacher friends would make the transition back into the real world such a positive experience for me, showering me each day with their generous spirits.

My prayers were answered with a welcoming place where I could thrive as I healed. These teachers will always hold a special place in my heart because of their humble, daily acts of kindness. As I was drowning in sorrow, they saved me from going under.

~

By the time Morgan passed away in the fall of 2006, I had gained broad experience as a career educator, teaching students from first grade through the university level. I began my career teaching elementary students in first, third, and fourth grades. Later I received my Gifted Education certification and taught gifted students during the last eight years before I retired from the local school system. I knew my strength was teaching advanced students, and I really enjoyed interacting with that group of students. They were not only smart but creative and driven to learn. I loved the challenge.

But in 2009, it was time for me to retire from the school system after thirty-two years of teaching. I was honored to be named Teacher of the Year for my district and receive semifinalist recognition at the state level.

The month after I retired from the school system, I took a job at the University of Memphis, where I started a second teaching career. I worked with education majors, mentoring them through their senior projects, a requirement for them to obtain their teaching license.

So close to graduation, these college seniors were focused and attentive. They also brought energy and excitement to my days as they launched their new careers. It was rewarding to be a part of their educational journeys.

I taught at the university level for thirteen years, with a total of forty-five years overall serving as a teacher. My longevity in education came from my love for the classroom. As a lifelong learner, I never faced the dreaded burnout that so many educators battle. I believe this was because I was always trying to learn new skills and change to various areas where I could continue to grow and learn.

Now my teaching skills are directed toward my Grace for Grief group. I launched the ministry to support parents who have lost children, but the group has offered layers of support for me too, as I continue the path of being a lifelong educator.

~

In the wake of grief, we need to look forward to the day we will venture out into the world again. But not too soon. We have the right to say "no, thank you" to invitations, especially during the first few months of grieving.

For example, a formal charity dinner took place two months after Morgan died. I didn't want to attend, and neither did my husband. We had not been out much in public since our loss, and facing a big crowd was the last thing we wanted.

However, some out-of-town friends were traveling in for the event, and we both wanted to spend time with them. When another friend encouraged us to attend, I knew her motives were pure. She thought it would be good for Mike and me to get out of the house and join our social circles again.

As it turned out, nothing could have been further from the truth.

We attended the charity function, and it was one of the most miserable evenings I can recall. The room was filled with couples in formal attire, and we saw hundreds of friends. Normally, we'd be eager to socialize, but that night, we did not want to engage in intimate conversations with any of them. It was too soon for us to be out in public, and neither of us was mentally prepared to share our sorrows with others. I was comfortable with our small group of close friends, but even they could sense that we were uncomfortable being out that night.

One friend described it best, saying, "I can see the sorrow in your eyes."

Mike and I were relieved when we could finally step away from the party and go home. It was a hard lesson. But I truly discovered how to listen to my instincts, especially when it came to going out in public again.

I finally figured out that I couldn't meet some schedule or live up to the expectations of others, but rather I needed to honor the rhythm of healing in my own time. Learning to say no, even to close friends, has saved me from other nights of suffering. Our true friends always understood.

At the same time, I would encourage others not to limit themselves. I thought about what Morgan would have wanted me to do at this stage of my life. Would she have wanted me to stay home and isolate myself from everyone? Sink into a depressed state and feed my misery? Or would she rather I go back to a job I loved and make a difference in the lives of my students?

Stepping out in faith can help us make the right decisions. With earnest prayer, we can feel at peace while navigating an otherwise stressful journey.

So today I will pick fresh, pink, fragrant roses from my garden.

I'll wear Morgan's signature pink color as I put my dress on in the morning.

I will dance and twirl to my favorite music: oldies and Motown hits.

Even today, life preservers show up at just the right time to save me from waves of melancholy. I have learned to trust in the greater community and remember I'm not alone on this journey through grief. When self-pity sets in, I fight against episodes of despair and the sorrowful thoughts that start to permeate my mind. I call my sisters to hear their comforting voices and laughter. I invite a friend over for a girls' wind-down Wednesday, our favorite midweek escape.

Moving forward, I allow no room in my day for doubt or depression. Instead, I yearn for the bountiful gifts of joy and happiness, just as Morgan would want me to do.

He heals the brokenhearted
and bandages their wounds.
He counts the stars
and names each one.
Our Lord is great and very powerful.
There is no limit to what he knows.
—Psalm 147:3–5

24

SAY HER NAME

Some people are so much sunlight to the square inch.
—Walt Whitman

All parents appreciate hearing stories about their children and their accomplishments. It's the same whether your child is here or in heaven. Some people are probably afraid to mention Morgan in case they upset me. But I take as much pride in hearing about Morgan as I do hearing about Kirk. Talking about her keeps her memory alive.

When others share their stories about Morgan, they offer us a window into her world. We're given a glimpse of a moment we might not have known about, and then we can share that experience with the person who tells us the story.

I cling to the stories people share, especially the ones I haven't heard before. Recently, one of Morgan's friends, Karen, told me about when she first met Morgan in the church children's choir when they were five or six.

"Morgan had the cutest outfits. They were like 3-D. Each outfit had a color scheme with printed leggings and a graphic of a girl on the top with a phone or something fun. I finally got up the courage to ask her where she got her clothes, and she didn't know, so we looked at the label, and it was Zoodles. I remember the day Mamaw brought home my first Zoodles outfit. I couldn't wait to wear it to church on Wednesday so Morgan could see it. We laughed and called ourselves the 'Zoodle girls' like it was a club. It's·wild to recall our first meeting, but Morgan was fun, and her energy was electric. I just wanted to follow her around."

Karen said she went to the same hairdresser as Morgan in middle school because of Morgan's long blond hair. "I wanted my hair just like hers. I can tell you, twenty-five years later, what she was wearing on the first day of middle school—white shorts and a pink top from Express. That was how memorable she was!"

I only recently heard the story about the "Zoodle girls" and smiled as I imagined the girls at that carefree, innocent age.

If you are a grieving parent who doesn't know how to respond when people bring up your child's name in conversation, I encourage you to accept those stories as gifts, as new ways to stay connected to your loved one. It's a blessing to know our children are not forgotten.

Yes, mentioning my child's name may make me tear up or smile, but not mentioning my child's name will break my heart.

As energetic as Morgan was, I was always finding ways to keep her engaged. From playing T-ball to soccer to dance to cheerleading, she was happiest when she was busy. We spent our summers at the swimming pool, starting at the baby pool, then advancing to the three-foot-deep pool, and finally to the adult and lap pools with the high dives.

Both Kirk and Morgan could swim at a young age, so I had my work cut out for me watching out for them in different pool areas. I finally put a big ribbon in Morgan's hair, so I could keep track of her bobbing around.

One of Kirk's favorite stories about Morgan was when she tried to go swimming in Elvis's pool during a visit to Memphis. That summer, her Aunt Denise was visiting with friends from Orlando, and they wanted to see Elvis's home, Graceland. So off we went for a day of discovery.

The tour included Elvis's airplane, the *Lisa Marie*, with huge seat belts across the king-size bed. The mansion at Graceland is a Colonial Revival home atop a hill, surrounded by rolling green pasture and a grove of shady oak trees. The white front gate of the home features musical notes on one side and a picture of Elvis on the other, with the wrought iron curving toward the front of the twenty-three-room house. No matter the time, day, or month, a crowd can always be found outside those gates, snapping photos and signing their names on the concrete sidewalks.

Once inside the home, the tour included only a few rooms open to the public. Morgan's favorite was the music room, with its vivid turquoise- and green-colored peacocks set in stained glass on each side of the doors. The house took us back to the sixties, with all the furnishings exactly as they were when Elvis lived there. Morgan enjoyed seeing the Jungle Room too, with green shag carpet on the floors and ceiling and Polynesian-style furniture. Kirk liked the blue-felt pool table in the playroom, complete with four hundred yards of pleated fabric draping the walls and ceilings in hues of bright blue, deep purple, and striking red.

Next was an impressive trophy gallery, which housed Grammy Awards and flashy outfits Elvis had worn while performing on stages around the world. Outside was the serene Meditation Garden and fountains, which serve as the resting place for Elvis and his family.

The final stop was a sparkling swimming pool, a welcome sight on that hot August day.

As Kirk tells it,

We were surrounded by crowds of tourists at the last stop of the tour, and Morgan let go of my mom's hand. I looked up and saw her running straight for the swimming pool. She ran under the velvet ropes and never looked back. I heard Morgan scream, 'Floaties, Mama!' Then she scurried toward the water's edge. Horrified, my mother and I grabbed her just as she breached the security line, ready to leap in for a dip. Everyone laughed, but I was so embarrassed. I was ready to exit quickly with all the commotion. But that was Morgan, always ready for the next adventure.

The docent and I were relieved that she had not managed to jump into the pool. Disappointed and in tears, Morgan never understood why the off-limits pool wasn't a perfect playground.

Her adventurous spirit was clear even at three years old, making it a challenge for us to keep up. She never had a dull moment and was always the life of the party. That was Morgan—a girl always in pursuit of fun.

We've told that story many times and laughed at her boldness. She wasn't impressed with the estate or the long tour, but that pool certainly captured her interest. She didn't care that the pool had belonged to Elvis. She just wanted to swim.

This is just one of the many stories we share with smiles as we honor Morgan's joyfully adventurous spirit. So I encourage you to decorate your loved one's watercolor memory with all the rich and vibrant stories of their life. Encourage others to say their name and share their memories, from childhood to the final moments. You may find that those people who knew them can tell you the most delightful tales and anecdotes that will bring a smile to your face.

I'm often reminded of a quote Morgan shared on her Facebook page: "Live life like it's going out of style."

What a way to live! Morgan taught us to appreciate the hidden blessings life has to offer. As Morgan knew, it's not about the final masterpiece but about the journey. We all need to enjoy the experience. We've learned the hard way that life can end without warning.

By telling stories and sharing memories of our loved ones, we can still enjoy life through their eyes, all while making every shared moment a celebration.

25

MODELING EXPERIMENT

You are made for sunshine.
—Unknown

As a teenager, Morgan had a modeling stint that lasted several years. Her dad and I were not excited about it, but she received good training from her modeling lessons in Memphis. If nothing else, she helped me with makeup and was always showing me new ways to dress stylishly.

My husband and I were both concerned about the images she might be asked to portray, so we always kept up with what she was working on. Our eyes opened wide when she was invited to work a runway modeling show in Dallas for the opening of the apparel market. Because she was only fifteen, there was no way we could let her go without us. Her dad and I flew to Dallas with her for the event.

Most of the clothes she would wear were provided at the show, but she needed an outfit of her own for the opening. Not knowing what to do, I went to a friend's dress shop, and she selected the perfect dress—a hot-pink silk gown by Dolce & Gabbana. However, I had sticker shock when I saw the price.

As Morgan beamed proudly at the gown's perfect fit, I didn't have the heart to tell her no. So I decided that this was a secret we'd keep between us, one that Dad did not have to know.

At the first rehearsal, Mike and I sat in the audience, and it seemed like we were the only parents around. I naively assumed the other girls were local, but we soon realized that no one was from Dallas. In fact, the girls had flown in from all over the country, and very few had been accompanied by parents or chaperones. Some of them were much younger than Morgan, and the situation horrified us.

Some girls had been doing this work for years, traveling to different cities without any supervision or protection. Mike and I both felt that Morgan was far too young to bear this responsibility by herself. Thankfully, she agreed.

As the week continued, Morgan did a fantastic job on the runway, using the skills she had learned in her classes at Memphis. The turn, the look, the expressionless gaze, were all practiced, and she had the walk down perfectly.

She also learned more about the world of modeling, hearing stories from young girls who'd already had plastic surgery to reshape themselves the way the agents thought they should look. Agencies tried to sign Morgan up all week, praising her high cheekbones and adding comments like "You can't buy those!" They also complimented her beautiful skin tone and her long blond hair. However, they were quick to suggest a nose job. "It might help to make it a little smaller," one said. Yes, she did have a McCarty nose, but I loved every inch of it and was offended that someone wanted to change our perfect daughter.

Thankfully, Morgan had a good attitude about it all. We laughed about the whole trip, but decided this might not be the avenue she would take.

Instead, she chose to work for an agency based in Nashville, and through them, she had chances to do some local modeling. She also got to be on CMT television shows as an extra and loved meeting country music stars.

Her favorite job was being a "seat filler" for the Country Music Awards. She got to wear her finest evening dresses and blingy jewelry and occupy the vacant seats while stars were on stage performing. She also did print modeling, but her strength was her height—five feet ten inches, or six feet one in heels—which made her ideal for runway work.

All through high school, Morgan would jump at the chance to work when the agent called, but the whole modeling stint phased out during her freshman year in college. She was called to work an awards show in Nashville but turned it down. "I don't think I can make it that night," she said. "I don't want to miss our sorority meeting."

I hung up the phone with a big hallelujah! The modeling hobby had run its course, and our worries were over. She'd rejected a glamorous night with Nashville's biggest stars to spend the evening at the Kappa Kappa Gamma sorority house with her friends instead. Music to my ears!

Morgan's beautiful hot-pink silk dress from her runway debut had one more appearance, but it was to be for all eternity.

My sister said, "I know she was a beautiful young lady, but she also had an inner beauty." Morgan was kind and thought of others more than herself.

I wish I could have shouted the same thing at the top of my lungs to all those people who admired her outer beauty. She was much more than just a pretty face. And it's still what I want the world to know about her now. Maybe that's why "Morgan stories" are like precious gems to me. I love hearing about all the ways Morgan touched so many lives. Any story shared fills me with incredible joy.

The adage that time heals all wounds simply does not apply to the loss of a child. We eventually learn to adjust to our child's absence, find a way to live through the pain and loss, but the suffering is always there and never fully goes away. Throughout your grief journey, you will learn to adapt.

My faith was instrumental in my healing process. Knowing Morgan was a Christian filled me with great peace, as I found comfort in knowing she was now in the arms of God. That belief alone made it easier to get up each morning, and still today, I find hope in knowing she is walking the runway in heaven.

Be humble under God's powerful hand so he will lift you up when the right time comes. Give all your worries to him, because he cares about you.

—1 Peter 5:6–7

26

DON'T COMPARE LOSSES

It's so easy to be there when it's all sunshine, but it really takes strength and courage to be there for each other during the dark times.
—Bindi Irwin

We live in a world where we want to avoid pain at all costs. Seeing our pain can cause the people around us to feel pain too. Our pain may make them feel uncomfortable because they don't know how to help us.

Their good intentions don't always translate into helpful words. Sometimes the things people say, even in kindness, leave me feeling misunderstood and a little bruised. Expressions like "I know how you feel," "Everything happens for a reason," "Just give it time," "God never gives us more than we can handle," "She's in a better place," or "Now God has another angel" can still sting our hearts, even when people mean to offer comfort.

Sometimes I want to snap back with the raw truth: "The better place would be with me! She should be here with her mother right now."

While I do believe Morgan is in heaven with God and that I'll see her again, those statements don't lessen my grief in any way.

Many people say things like, "I'm thinking of you," and I appreciate those comments. However, it would be wonderful to hear, instead, "We are remembering and missing Morgan today." Saying her name brings my child into the present.

Just as it is impossible to explain childbirth to a woman who has never given birth, it is impossible to explain the loss of a child to a person who has never lost a child. People cannot relate to what we are going through. Trying to sympathize with us by comparing the loss of an elderly parent, grandparent, or worse...a pet...feels unfathomable.

Losing a pet cannot possibly be compared to losing a child, yet people have said that to me and to many of my friends who've faced the same circumstances.

Sometimes it's hard for me to bite my tongue. I want to say, "Really? You can't be serious!"

Of course, we love our pets as much as anyone does, but the absurdity of the comment would be almost laughable if the person were not so serious in equating the grief of losing a pet with losing a child.

My parents and grandparents, whom I adored, were hard for me to lose, but this type of death fit the natural order of life. They had lived long, full lives, and we all expect to go through this kind of loss eventually.

However, no one expects to go through the death of a child. It's out of order. It stops you in your tracks. Chaos disrupts the way life is supposed to play out, and it leaves us picking up the pieces. There are no words from philosophers, therapists, or psychologists to make sense of that kind of grief. Instead, send me a friend who will simply hold my hand, listen to me, help with the dishes, and give me ice cream.

For grieving parents, grief hides just under the surface. Even in happy moments, the recurring tide of grief threatens to resurface.

As I told my husband, "It is always present, but not always seen. We mask our grief until we can't. It's a Jekyll-and-Hyde existence. I can be in the depths of despair one moment and then rise like a shining sun the next, filled with precious and blessed memories as I find myself smiling again."

This is the ebb and flow of a bereaved parent's life. Don't ever think someone is over the death of a child. There is no cure for that kind of loss. Like the glistening tide, grief appears again and again. It goes out to reveal raw feelings; then, in an instant, the waves come back to revitalize your soul.

As time passes, I am glad to have more days of the tide coming in and bringing joy and hope and laughter into my life. I've learned over the years to be steady on my feet at the beach. The ocean is tricky, and we never know when the next wave will knock us down. Rip currents can pull us out, drawing us away from the shore, far out to the treacherous sea of despair. Or, the jellyfish can wash up on the sand, their tentacles releasing their wrenching poison—grief.

I remain on guard against this waxing and waning of life. Experience teaches us to be ready for not only the gleam and glisten of calm waters, but also for the grim and raging parts as well.

27

THE TRIAL

May the sunshine of comfort shine through the gloom and despair.
—Anonymous

Nine months after her death, the trial for Morgan's hit-and-run driver was scheduled to begin. This was a grueling process to withstand. My emotions were high, as I had to relive the scene over and over in my mind.

At that point in my grief journey, I was feeling pure rage. Morgan's life had been cut short not by illness, but because someone had intentionally chosen not to value her life. Not only had he driven while under the influence, but he'd also deliberately left my child severely injured at the scene and had taken no accountability for his destructive actions.

This was no innocent mistake. This was no accident. This was a cold-hearted act that ended Morgan's beautiful life for no reason other than one person's selfish behavior. It may not have been premeditated, but to me, it was murder. How dare someone take my child away from me!

No excuse for her death would be good enough.

We had waited all these months, and now we were finally going to face the person who had done this horrific deed. The buildup was almost more than I could stand.

Taking a deep breath, I told my husband, "At this point, I just want the person responsible to pay for what he did. I just want it to be over with."

We made our way to the Knoxville courthouse as a united family, only to be met with television and radio journalists thrusting microphones into our faces. Reporters demanded statements, which I could not bear to give.

"No comment" was my response, my heart racing as we were escorted through the crowds.

Throngs of people had packed the courthouse doors, and cameras flashed at us from all directions. We kept our heads down and avoided eye contact. The police had to clear a path for our family to enter.

The death of a college student in a university town had made headlines at the time of Morgan's passing, and it was front-page news that day too. Media outlets were eager to follow up on the story. I understood their jobs, but I was not in a state of mind to be interviewed on camera. I just wanted to get through the trial and have this grueling process end as soon as possible.

When I entered the courtroom, an oppressive force crushed my chest, making breathing difficult. This had happened to me before, and I knew what was happening. With such intense pressure on my chest, it almost felt like I was having a heart attack. I felt, with my whole body, a dark and evil presence, as if I were being attacked by forces I couldn't control. My spiritual gift of discernment enabled me to separate good from evil, truth from falsehood, wisdom from foolishness. Most of the time, it came as a subtle thought or idea, or sometimes a gentle nudge to get my attention when a person near me meant harm. But it has also happened in various locations or buildings.

Years earlier, while visiting Stonehenge in England, I'd had the same uneasy feeling, and I knew that evil things had happened on that site. I felt chilled, and the hair on my arms stood up. As we approached the monuments, I'd even asked my fellow travelers, "Do you sense that uneasy feeling of clammy coldness?"

No one seemed to know what I meant, so I knew then it was my feeling alone. At that time, visitors could walk all the way through and between the stones and touch them, with no fence keeping guests at a distance. The eerie feeling only left when I boarded the bus and left the area.

I had sensed the same evil presence at the Colosseum in Rome. An eerie feeling came over me, and I was again the only person in my group who felt it. The horrific, murderous past of this place manifested itself in my uneasiness. I quickly exited the building, and my abnormal feelings vanished.

In the courthouse, I could not simply leave the building. Instead, as that heavy force of pressure descended on my chest, I prayed to escape this person's presence quickly.

I had brought one of Morgan's purses with me to the courtroom that day. The smell of fragrant cologne wafted from her handbag, which I clutched close to me. "I want to bring her purse with me today," I'd told Mike. "I want something of hers near so I can feel her presence."

As Helen Keller said, "Smell is a potent wizard that transports us across thousands of miles and all the years we have lived." Indeed, the restorative comfort and power of Morgan's fragrance surrounded me that day.

The trial started with a not guilty plea from the driver. He sat on the opposite side of the courtroom, but I could not look at him. Instead, I stared ahead, concentrating on the lawyer's words: "We have an eyewitness to the wreck and crime that night."

"Thank goodness for the young man who was with Morgan," Mike whispered. "He's able to identify the driver and recount exactly what happened."

With a heavy heart, I sighed. "Yes, this will all be over today."

Another suspect had been brought in earlier in the week. She'd reportedly been in the car that had hit Morgan, and she willingly reported the details to the police. She'd also verified the name of the man who'd been driving the car.

Apparently, the woman and the forty-something-year-old male driver had been leaving a party, going to buy more drugs, when they'd driven through the University of Tennessee campus. On the way, they hit Morgan as she crossed the street. Instead of stopping or calling for help, they'd just kept driving.

Morgan was one block from her home.

So, so close.

Unfortunately, the female informant had not shown up to testify at the trial, so the jury had to depend solely on the eyewitness testimony of the young man who'd been walking with Morgan that night.

Knoxville police were surprised the informant had not shown up because she could have collected a big reward—twenty thousand dollars. After searching for her for months, the police had still been unable to locate her. She had disappeared.

Because the driver had not been arrested until six days after Morgan's death, no drugs were found in his system, and it could not be proven that he had been driving under the influence that night. He did receive a guilty verdict, but much to our dismay, he was sentenced to less than three years in prison, the maximum allowed by Tennessee law at that time.

My eyes flashed with anger. "Not even three years? How can this be?"

Our close friend and attorney, Alan, explained that the maximum sentencing would be light because of the way the law was written.

I hit my fist on the table. "Well then, we need to change the law!"

And we started thinking about strengthening the law that day.

Kirk and I were both relieved and angry about the whole proceeding. Mike, in his wisdom, was steadier. As we left the courtroom, he told us, "We are leaving this right here on the courthouse steps. This is not going to eat away at us for the rest of our lives. We are going to look at the best way to honor and remember Morgan."

And that's what we did.

We walked away and left the driver's name behind. We only took Morgan with us.

We walked away and closed that chapter of our lives. The focus of our future would not be on what we had just endured. Instead, we chose to celebrate the twenty years of precious memories we had of Morgan. In that moment, Mike encouraged us to release the pain and to choose joy again—to choose love.

So far, we've survived 100 percent of our worst days.

Morgan's friends comforted and surrounded us with support during the painful trial and afterward. Her roommate and friend, Katey, reflected on her relationship with Morgan.

When Morgan and I became friends, we were inseparable, even though Morgan was a grade older than me. Being friends with Morgan, you were one of the 'cool kids,' because everyone loved being around her. She was so much fun. I remember always going over to her house to get ready for a night out with friends, and Morgan would help me dress to a T. Then she would go into one of her many jewelry boxes and find the best jewelry to add to my outfit. She was always so generous, letting friends borrow clothes or jewelry. She loved helping people feel good.

While loving girly things, Morgan was not afraid of a little dirt. We loved going out to the country with our friends to ride on four-wheelers, shoot skeet, and just enjoy nature. We both were comfortable going from high heels to barefoot in the mud. I can say that during the time I spent with her, I can't remember a single argument between girlfriends. We just went together that easily. She was my very best friend.

ONE OF THE best qualities about Morgan was her ability to never judge others. She never judged me for the poor teenage decisions I made growing up. She was always there to support me or cheer me on, saying, 'You only live once.' She was my biggest cheerleader, because in life, sometimes we don't always need a coach, we just need that one person to be there for us while we learn from our own mistakes. As I learned from my own experiences in life, Morgan was my one person and always will be. I am grateful to have known her and miss Morgan's friendship every day. She was truly one of a kind and impossible to replace.

So don't worry, because I am with you.
Don't be afraid, because I am your God.
I will make you strong and will help you;
I will support you with my right hand that saves you.
—Isaiah 41:10

28

THE MCCARTY BILL

Keep your face always toward the sunshine, and shadows will fall behind you.
—M.B. Whitman

While watching local television news in June 2007, I heard Senator Don McLeary announce that he was introducing the McCarty-Britt bill to strengthen the hit-and-run law in the state of Tennessee. Surprised by his gesture, I started calling him to find out about the bill and how we could help.

Our community had been deeply affected by Morgan's death in September 2006, when she was killed by a hit-and-run driver. Just a week after her death, Martha Britt, a beloved school principal, and her husband, Tom, were out for a morning walk when they were hit by a driver who also left the scene. Martha did not survive, and her husband, Tom, remained critically injured for more than a year.

These tragic events were devastating to our Jackson community, as we mourned the loss of two beloved citizens within just one week. The bill had been named to honor Morgan and Martha, in hopes of changing the law and delivering stiffer penalties to hit-and-run drivers. As the laws in the state of Tennessee stood at that time, the lax sentencing didn't fit the crime and did nothing to protect innocent victims of these tragedies.

As months went by, Senator Don McLeary lost the election, and Senator Lowe Finney introduced the bill, as did Representative Jimmy Eldridge in the House. I was eager to help in any way I could to see this bill pass.

I had no experience in politics, but I jumped in with both feet and fought passionately in support of the bill. I traveled to Nashville and met with representatives and senators at the Tennessee State Capitol. I spoke personally to everyone who would meet with me, hoping I could help them put a name and face to the cause. I sent emails and called as many legislators as I could reach, asking for their support.

About every six weeks, the bill was brought up for consideration in the Senate Judiciary Committee, and I would travel to Nashville each time to speak to the committee members in person. The late Martha Britt, whose name was also on the bill, had been married to a local television journalist, and Tom made sure to send a camera crew with me each time for press coverage.

A little nervous about talking to the Senate committee, I found my heart racing and hands trembling as I prepared to speak at the podium. "I hope my emotions don't take over today," I told Mike. "I need to be clear about our message and express how important this bill could be for other victims' families."

Morgan was at the very heart of our appeal, and I wanted to communicate my concerns clearly. My emotions fueled my voice as I boldly expressed the need to strengthen the hit-and-run laws in our state. I grew more confident and more aggressive as I relayed Morgan's case.

"Last September, at the University of Tennessee campus, the person responsible for hitting and leaving my daughter was caught and given the maximum sentence, which only lasted one and a half years. I did not feel like justice was served in her case."

I stressed the need to make the jail sentences longer. I hoped the bill could help prevent a tragedy such as hers from happening to another innocent person and family.

"Our family has been torn apart, and my young, twenty-year-old daughter, who had her whole life ahead of her, was taken away in a callous act. She was a junior enjoying her college years when, out of the blue, a car came and claimed her life. No more school, no more friends, and certainly no more future for her precious life. My family and I ask that you consider voting for this bill to let criminals know the state of Tennessee does not condone or tolerate hit-and-run drivers. If one other family can be spared the horrors of losing a child, all our efforts would be worth it. Thank you."

Feeling empowered that I had done something for my daughter, I confidently walked out of the Senate chamber with the film crew in tow. This was one mother who meant business.

Thousands of people signed petitions in support of the bill, and they were hand-delivered to the Capitol. Various legislators received a stream of phone calls and emails daily. We led a continuous push from September 2007 to April 2008 when the legislature was back in session. We had constituents from all over the state call their representatives to help support the bill. Hundreds of supportive friends joined us in pleading with our lawmakers to rewrite the offense of leaving the scene of an accident and increase penalties depending upon the culpability of the driver, the degree of harm, and the location of the accident.

Along with our bill came a funding requirement to pay for longer sentences. I had been warned by Representative Eldridge that bills with a fiscal note were not likely to pass because of funding constraints. That spring he explained, "We can start working on the bill again in the fall when the Tennessee General Assembly meets for the new session. I am not giving up."

"Neither am I," I told him. As disappointed as I was by the delays, I was already making plans for the fall session. A new wave of energy came over me. I was on a mission.

I pointed out to Mike, "This bill may have Morgan's name on it, but it's really for the others who will come after her. It's so those families can find justice."

He agreed. "We just need to keep the momentum up and continue the push in the fall."

My family and friends were ready to regroup and start again when the phone rang. I was caught off guard when Representative Eldridge exclaimed, "The bill is passing!"

I immediately burst into tears, not quite believing what I had heard. We both were crying on the phone, and I was jumping up and down with excitement.

Astonished at the quick turnaround, I asked for more information. "What happened with the funding?"

"The money has been appropriated, and the bill will go to the floor for a final vote on May 20," he explained.

I was ecstatic and appreciative of all his dedication and hard work. The long, toilsome journey for House Bill 852 and Senate Bill 1054 was finally over.

Soon, Mike and I were invited to appear on the House floor in Nashville to observe the bill being officially voted into law. On June 3, 2008, we entered the Capitol with the camera crew from WBBJ television. We were eager to capture the big moment.

The day was full of incredible happiness as well as agony. When we arrived, I looked around at the hundreds of people attending the session, thrilled to be included.

Representatives and senators from both sides of the aisle—Democrats and Republicans alike—had backed the bill. When the bill was read, and we saw "McCarty-Britt bill" appear on the ticker-tape display, it was a proud moment for all of us.

I was given the privilege of pushing the vote button at Representative Eldridge's desk as the bill came up for its final vote.

My eyes filled with tears as I pressed the button.

While it was certainly a victory for our persistence and hard work, it also left a void because no amount of legislation would help Morgan. Our case was over. And the driver involved would not receive a second sentence with harsher penalties for his crime. But I found great relief in knowing this law would help the next hit-and-run victim's family seek justice. Thanks to a community's determination, we had strengthened the laws, paving the way for longer jail sentences, which we hoped would make the next driver think twice before leaving the scene of the crime.

A lot of work and one mother's determination had finally paid off when the McCarty-Britt bill was signed into law.

This was one thing I felt I could do in Morgan's name that would have some meaning to us and to others across the state who faced our same circumstances.

Never underestimate mothers.

Mothers never give up.

Back at home, I was pleased to learn that Ginger, a young neighbor friend of ours, had created MLM decals and passed them out to the younger set of friends and family for their cars. They had no date or name—just Morgan's initials in hot pink.

The generous gesture touched my heart, but my grief was still too raw in those early days to put the sticker on my car. I told Kirk, "It's too tough to see that every day. I won't be able to explain to anyone who asks about it. It's just too difficult right now."

Kirk nodded in agreement, saying, "I feel the same way," as he took a decal for his mirror at home.

In time, I grew used to seeing the decals on friends' cars as they traveled through town. I told my sister, Donna, "The decals make me smile now. They're such a gentle reminder that people cared about her."

As the years passed, I saw fewer and fewer stickers as cars were sold and the stickers went with them. But our neighbors, Susan and Joey, Ginger's parents, still had the white van with the sticker displayed in the back window. The last one standing.

I began to look for it in our neighborhood and would ask Mike, "Look to see if Morgan's sticker is still on the window," and sure enough, it was always still there.

"I'm glad we have one left to see," I would say, beaming.

But time keeps passing.

Twelve years later, our neighbors replaced their van, and the last of the decals was gone. It was a sad moment. All that is left now is the memory of the goodness of others and a kind act that extended Morgan's presence in our lives.

But that was not the end of the story.

The van was purchased by a New Yorker who collected all types of vehicles. When his relative arrived to pick up the van, he asked about the MLM sticker and heard Morgan's story. The man said his relative owned a car museum in New York and would proudly display Morgan's sticker as part of the van's history. Weeks later, true to his word, he sent a picture of the van on display in the museum, with the decal still on the back. This thoughtful gesture gave me comfort. The hot-pink decal was still being seen hundreds of miles away in honor of Morgan.

What wonderful tributes to our daughter. Whether it was a bill in her name or a simple decal placed on the back of a vehicle, Morgan's memory continues to live on in our hearts and minds.

29

VISION TO REALITY

The glow of the setting sun kisses life's hurts away.
—Unknown

Days before Morgan's funeral, during a somber gathering of close friends on our screened porch, we came up with the concept of the Morgan McCarty Memorial Scholarship Foundation. As soon as the group had agreed, our close friend Danny hurried to the phone and called the bank to set up an account.

Once the cards were printed, the first gifts were designated as memorial donations, and family and friends generously gave in Morgan's memory. Soon after the funeral, ideas started springing up about ways to fund scholarships for the long term. Because we had a group of golfing friends, it was only natural to talk about a fundraising tournament.

Lucinda said excitedly, "We can have an annual golf tournament to raise money for the scholarships."

The following August, friends and family gathered to play in the first Morgan Leah McCarty Golf Classic. We learned many lessons during that debut tournament, with one being *not* to play in August in Tennessee.

The heat was intense, but not one participant mentioned it. We had two full flights, but all the golfers simply accepted our water and iced towels with no complaints. Our family felt so deeply supported by everyone who came.

After that first year, we moved the tournament to September, when the temperatures are a little cooler. This made a big difference. And, since it is also a month with little rain, we've never had to cancel in all our nineteen years.

Although we had two full flights of golfers eager to play that first year, we needed a way to get the word out to the community. Our other friend, Danny, designed a brochure for the second year, with Morgan's photo on the front. I chose one of her senior pictures taken in Destin, Florida, and we still use that photo for current tournament materials.

That first year, we formed a board of directors and drew up a plan to achieve 501(c)(3) charitable foundation status. With the help of our lawyer friends, Teresa and Alan, we created bylaws and submitted paperwork. We received approval just ten months later. Our proceeds funded college scholarships.

In the first two years, we gave $500 and then $1,000 scholarships to students at the University of Tennessee. However, we realized our donors were primarily local West Tennessee residents who played in and attended our events. At that point, we changed the scholarship criteria to be limited to students in West Tennessee, regardless of where they chose to attend college.

Through the years, we've hosted dances with silent and live auctions, some drawing more than three hundred attendees. We rented a music venue, Live at the Barn, and featured local musicians. We even had a mystery dinner, where actors portrayed characters and gradually revealed a hilarious storyline. It seemed like whatever event we advertised for Morgan's scholarship fund, friends, family, and the public would come.

"I attribute the success of our events to Morgan's charismatic personality and her long-range reach of friends. What a blessing that people have consistently supported us in every fundraiser!" Donna said.

A flourishing fundraising effort allowed us to significantly increase the scholarship amounts awarded to deserving students. We grew from one student to two, then to four students each year. As the fund became endowed, we dropped most of our fundraising efforts except the golf classic. Every year, Mike asks the board of directors if they want to continue with the golf tournament, and he's always met with a resounding "yes!" Our husbands just don't want to give it up.

After years of putting on this tournament, we have simplified the planning process to only about two meetings a year. We've managed to streamline the entire event, orchestrating more than eighty golfers on tournament day each year.

Everybody has a job. Alan sets up the teams. Ed creates signs. Debbie, Ginger, and Paula manage lunch, with Frank and John cooking the barbecue. Greg is always in charge of getting a local dealership to provide a car for a hole-in-one giveaway. Molly, Elizabeth, Paula, and countless friends help by sitting at the prize holes on the golf course. Jerri Sue, Michelle, Lisa, and Tracy, along with others in the community, take care of donated golf prizes. Danny helps with drinks and advertising, and the rest of the board members reach out to local businesses to secure donations and prizes. My two sisters, Donna and Kandy, oversee checking in teams on the day of the tournament and help make sure everything runs smoothly.

The day after each golf tournament, we critique the event and share ideas on how to make it better the next year. Today, we have scaled back the tournament to one flight, instead of one in the morning and one in the afternoon. We take pride in knowing 100 percent of the money raised goes to the scholarship fund. Our wonderful barbecue lunch, our trophies, and all the prizes are donated each year.

This past year, we awarded $7,500 each to four area scholarship recipients for a total of $30,000 for their college expenses. Because we receive many applications, our scholarship committee screens for students with good academic standing, as well as financial need. For the past twelve years, we have also awarded, through the Jackson-Madison County Sports Hall of Fame, a $1,000 scholarship to a deserving high school athlete.

The scholarships have been a blessing, and so many of the recipients over the past seventeen years have called and written letters to express their appreciation. Through tears of gratitude, one parent cried, "I just lost my job, and this enables my daughter to attend school."

Another family shared, "I had medical bills from an injury, and money was so tight I could not afford the college tuition until we received this scholarship."

And still another student recipient told me, "I am working to help support two siblings and provide for their basic needs. Working part-time, I would not be able to go to college without this scholarship."

It's not unusual to receive phone calls from the parents of the students telling us with heartfelt thanks and tears how the money was going to help and how much they appreciated the scholarship for their child. It is also rewarding to be on the giving end of a scholarship and see firsthand how financial assistance can change lives.

The golf weekend has become a family reunion, with relatives coming home to help and participate in the weekend. It's a bittersweet weekend for the McCarty family. We always have sad moments because Morgan is not here with us, but we are grateful for the glorious memories of our daughter and the legacy of helping others in her memory.

We thought the golf classic would last a year or two at the most, and never dreamed we would be able to help so many deserving students along the way. Much to our surprise, 2026 will be the 20th Annual Morgan McCarty Golf Classic.

This could never have happened without our friends and family helping to bring this idea to life during our toughest season and remaining loyal to our cause. We have been blessed with the most incredible friends imaginable.

For it is in giving that we receive.
—Attributed to St. Francis

One of the most captivating places Morgan and I visited was the quaint town of Assisi, Italy.

I can still picture the day perfectly. It was a beautiful June morning with bright blue skies in the central Italian region of Umbria. Prosperous fields of olive trees and lush vineyards dotted the winding banks of the Tiber River. We were driving along the flat terrain when Morgan pointed miles into the distance and said, "Look ahead at that town rising out of the hills. It looks like it appeared out of nowhere."

Ahead of us, a well-preserved medieval town could have been from a fairy tale. The postcard-like village charmed us with its brightly colored stucco and the aromas of freshly baked bread and grilled lamb wafting through the open windows of bakeries and restaurants.

After stopping to look in the shops, I suggested we find a café for lunch.

"Yes! I'm starving," laughed Morgan. "We'll need energy to climb up that winding, cobblestone road to the basilica."

After weighing our many choices, we decided on a local restaurant with a swinging white sign that displayed its specials for the day in Italian. Inside the arched doorway, we picked a side table with a white-linen tablecloth, and an older lady promptly brought us hot bread with olive oil. The white domed ceiling floated above us like a cloud and made the room feel intimate and close. A bottle of red wine and a bottle of still water stood in the center of the table so we could serve ourselves.

"No paper napkins here," I noted, admiring how the casual lunches we enjoyed at home could not compare to the formality of this small Italian eatery.

In broken English, the waiter described unique delicacies such as stewed snails, fried goose, and boar stew.

"I'm not feeling brave enough for that! Not trying snails, goose, or boar today," Morgan said, laughing.

After a few more recommendations, we settled on *Porchetta di Costano,* and we were not disappointed by the fragrance of the spit-roasted pork dish or the rich flavors of the deep-red sauce.

We were on a tight schedule, especially if we wanted to explore the town and visit the famous church on the hill. But as we started to leave, the waiter encouraged us to linger through the afternoon. "You tourists are always in a hurry. Stay and enjoy more wine. Dessert!"

"We're with a tour group," I explained, "We really would like to stay longer, but we're eager to see the beautiful town. *Grazie* for a lovely lunch."

Smiling, Morgan and I linked arms and hurried out of the café to browse local artisan shops selling crafts, religious jewelry, handmade pottery, and linens with festive flowers. As we strolled up the curved street, the fragrance of the nearby chocolate factory filled the ancient community.

"Mom, we didn't have time to have dessert at the café," Morgan announced, eyeing the chocolate store suggestively.

We couldn't resist, so we stopped in front of a medieval arched doorway at the Divine Chocolate shop to buy some dark chocolate, or "divine food," as advertised.

The arched wooden door invited us into a world of heavenly smells. Signs advertised handmade chocolate, and we were drawn to their *baci*. Baci means kisses in Italian, and the candy was the Italian version of a chocolate kiss. These yummy delights contained hazelnut and chocolate paste with a whole hazelnut on top, all covered in dark chocolate. With a tin of Italian kisses, we continued up the steep hill, where we met Franciscan monks in long, black robes with coarse-rope belts. They mingled and discussed the daily news with pilgrims who sat nonchalantly near a trickling fountain in the middle of the square.

We continued along the well-worn ancient street to the top of the city, where the Basilica of St. Francis impressed us with its Italian Gothic architecture, lofty arcades, and buttresses, all constructed in the early thirteenth century. Above us, the freestanding bell tower clanged as the church's arched windows donned paint colors that made them look like puffy pillows of white.

Perhaps what impressed us most were the twenty-eight spellbinding frescoes that depicted St. Francis's life along the basilica walls beneath the dazzling blue lapis ceiling. Through the ornate frescoes, we learned more about St Francis's ministry of helping the underprivileged, as well as his care for nature and animals.

"I've never seen such brilliant colors in a painting before," Morgan said, as we gazed up at the arched ceiling panels.

"At the time, most of the population could not read," the tour guide explained. "The common people could learn by viewing these magnificent frescoes as the stories were shared."

"Each section is more colorful than the next," I affirmed, as the breathtaking artworks made my spirits soar.

By the time Morgan and I left, we had gained a great appreciation for the skilled artisans who had created these scenes seven hundred years earlier. As we exited the basilica, we were met with the jubilant echo of bells announcing a wedding. The blushing bride and her groom waved to the crowd as they emerged from the church. The groom lifted his bride onto the back of a braying donkey, and off they went down the winding hill with the beautiful white dress trailing behind her. The wedding party tossed flowers and cheered as the happy couple meandered through the streets.

Morgan cried out, "How cool was that? We got to see an Assisi wedding."

Girls from the wedding party rushed to us and handed out flowers to throw as the couple rode by on the donkey, waving to the crowd.

"I feel like we're part of the wedding," Morgan beamed.

"Yes. We're lucky to be here today."

"Aww, Mom, I feel the same way," she said as she hugged me. "I'm so glad we're here together."

After looking out over the city, Morgan said, "I'll always remember the difference St. Francis made. Just look at what he started so long ago, and his teachings are still being followed. Look at all the monks and pilgrims who have come to worship in his church today. It's amazing."

"I agree. St. Francis gave up his wealth to live in poverty and help others. As one of Italy's patron saints, his followers still flock to see his birthplace."

As we were leaving, we were on a mission to find just the right souvenir treasure from Assisi. With her eyes full of wonder, Morgan smiled at all the choices. "I think I'll get this silver necklace," she said, holding up a charm that featured St. Francis blessing the animals.

After we returned home from Europe, Morgan wore that necklace every day to remind her of the trip and the ministry St. Francis had started there.

Morgan would be pleased with the scholarship that we founded in her memory, a meaningful way to honor her determination to help others. Morgan had always cared about service, so she enjoyed serving others through ministry, church camps, and community projects. She understood that sometimes you get more by helping others, especially those who are less fortunate.

Morgan had accumulated more than one thousand volunteer hours while in high school, choosing to dedicate her time and energy to numerous local charities. She was focused on her community, and this kind of service work was something she wanted to do, not something she had to do.

Even as a ten-year-old child, Morgan was driven to help others. As a school project, she started a pet-sitting service for the neighborhood and let neighbors know she could pet-sit while they were away. She printed cards and delivered them to families with pets.

I was proud she'd thought of the idea on her own and had followed through. Morgan was happiest staying busy and helping others in the process.

She also helped with our youth group at the Reelfoot Rural Ministry. The ministry serves families with numerous needs in one of the poorest counties in Tennessee. Morgan joined her peers and spent her weekends tearing down a dilapidated porch and rebuilding it for a family. They also replaced the kitchen floor that had been so worn down that a gaping hole exposed the ground underneath. Just the thought of people living in such crumbling homes was a shock to Morgan and to many of her friends. She never again took for granted her ability to come home to a safe shelter where she'd never had to worry about falling through the floor or having to walk up wooden planks just to enter the house.

That summer project took a lot of hard work, but it brought a great reward—the family's tremendous gratitude for the home improvements.

Exhausted from toiling in the July heat, Morgan explained, "The work was hard, but we made a difference for the families we helped. It was worth sleeping on the community center floor and eating peanut butter and jelly sandwiches."

Morgan knew that giving her time to help others was a privilege. She believed we are called to give a hand to those less fortunate, and she would be honored to know about the students who have been helped by The Morgan Leah McCarty Memorial Scholarship Foundation.

Many of those students would not have been able to attend college without her scholarship, a gift that has become a lifeline for them to advance their education and improve their lives. Today, as I think of all the students who have benefited from Morgan's scholarship fund, I'm reminded that it was far, far away in the quaint little town of Assisi, where Morgan first learned St. Francis's lesson.

"For it is in the giving we receive."

30

GRACE FOR GRIEF GROUP IS BORN

Those who bring sunshine to the lives of others cannot keep it from themselves.

—J. M. Barrie

An early understanding of grief came from meeting other bereaved parents, and their stories deeply resonated with me during my own family's journey. Witnessing their experiences provided hope and a sense of possibility—proof that it was possible to survive such excruciating loss. Inspired by these role models, I felt a growing responsibility to offer comfort to others facing similar tragedies.

Whenever I learned of a friend experiencing loss, I was compelled to visit, offering presence and a simple hug. Over time, my husband and I were contacted by friends seeking support for their acquaintances who had lost children. We reached out to these families, together and individually, providing the understanding and reassurance we ourselves had once needed. This felt like a calling from God, one I was meant to answer.

Gradually, I realized there were no local support groups for bereaved parents. While general grief classes existed, none addressed the unique experience of losing a child. The idea of starting a group lingered, but I hesitated, citing work and uncertainty about where to begin. I would argue with myself that I was too busy and did not have the time or skills to begin such a group. As the months passed, the idea kept coming back. Still, I found plenty of excuses not to see it through.

Finally, I went to my minister, Eddie, and told him about my idea.

"It keeps popping up in my head," I explained. "My main reason not to start a group is time. I am so busy teaching at the University of Memphis. Some days, I'm in schools observing student teachers all over West Tennessee. But despite how busy I am, the idea will not go away."

He replied, "That's your answer. It is meant for you to do this. God is not letting go of this idea for you."

When he gave me his blessing to hold a monthly meeting at the church, I had no more excuses. I started by reaching out to friends who had lost their own children. Many expressed interest right away, and the news quickly spread.

At our first meeting, several of the mothers confided that they had been looking for a place to express their feelings where people would understand.

And that's exactly what we created: a safe space where grieving parents could express feelings among those who understood this painful journey.

One friend, Sherry, had been attending a general grief group. When she attended our meeting, she shared, "It's not the same grief to lose a child as to lose a parent or spouse. It's simply different. This is a group that understands what it is like to lose a child. This group is the support I need to get through my grief."

We created a list of our children's birthdays and other important dates to honor the lives of those we grieved. We all knew how hard those days could be, and it helped to have friends with us through those landmark days. We bonded during that first meeting and continue to meet all these years later. We are still there to support each other and listen when needed.

Finding a support group can help with the healing process. Sharing grief experiences with others allows for mutual understanding and comfort, reminding us that we're not alone.

In the seven years since we started our group, we have learned that it doesn't matter how old our children were or how they died. We are all living with the same heartbreak of grieving a lost child. Some parents who come lost their children more than thirty years ago. Grief is still with them, even though they have learned to go on with their lives. Seeing how others deal with their pain provides helpful models of hope and resilience, inspiring fellow parents to continue with their lives too, even when it seems impossible to go on.

We have prayed over approaching anniversaries and holidays. One woman had a trial coming up for the man who struck and killed her son. It was postponed several times, and the emotional delays were difficult for her. When others shared their experiences with trials, she was comforted by understanding what to expect.

Just knowing there is a group of people praying for your strength can be a powerful gift.

What a blessing this group has been in my life! I've made new friends and formed deep bonds with these women. We go out to eat, laugh, cry, and genuinely care about each other. Becoming a bereaved parent is certainly not a group any of us would want to join, but this group has become such a vital resource for all of us. We offer support to one another as we honor and remember our children.

I celebrate how far many of our members have come on their grief journeys. Some could not get out of their houses or go anywhere in public without crying. With the support of each other, we are able as a group to embrace our good memories and also share our heartaches. I also learned that all mourners need a break from time to time. It's okay to smile, accept invitations to go out, and laugh without feeling guilty. As normalcy returns to our lives, we have a support group that shows up, listens, and understands.

Just being there for others is a treasured gift for all.

Now, as a certified grief counselor, I've seen group members struggling with severe depression and not progressing toward healing. I have given them the names of therapists and asked them to seek professional help. Anyone can face real struggles along the grief journey, and depression can lead to a downward spiral. We may get stuck in one stage and struggle to progress through the remaining stages of grief. This is dangerous and can lead to prolonged self-pity, despair, and harmful withdrawal from society.

Helen Keller, who was blind and deaf, remarked, "Keep your face to sunshine and you cannot see the shadows."

Without seeing the sun, Helen Keller could obviously still feel its warmth and power. She was a courageous person to not dwell on her life's difficulties, but instead reportedly focused on the positive parts of her life. This spirit helped her to stay out of the depths of darkness and live life to its fullest.

In grief, it is easy to dwell so much on what we have lost that we lose sight of what we still have. We can lose precious time by burying ourselves in the darkness of grief. Helen Keller reminds us all that it's important to come out into the sunshine of the day.

My heart hurts for every person's grief journey, but the scariest thing is to see people retreat to the confines of their sorrow and not engage with others. Nourishing grief and sadness is self-defeating and can become emotionally dangerous.

At one of our recent grief group meetings, I said, "I pray that people stuck in that deep hole of grief and depression will ask for an authority higher than themselves to lift them out of their pit of despair."

Today, I pray the same for each of you reading this book.

Moving through each stage can be difficult, so I encourage you to focus on one step at a time and not try to see too far ahead.

Over our time together, our group has journaled, made creative art that reminds us of our children, used music as a creative device, built serenity gardens at Easter, welcomed speakers on the stages of grief, written letters to our late children, shared books that were helpful, looked for places to get involved in the community, and attended local plays. With joy, we meet each month to check on one another and to fill each other's lives with meaningful conversation and laughter—yes, laughter. Sometimes encouragement is needed, sometimes cheering up is needed, sometimes just talking is needed. We meet each other wherever we are in the moment.

When we welcome a newcomer to the group, I say, "The reality is that unless you have walked this path, you will never understand. But these ladies do understand."

We are soulmates for life.

Even though my group is all women, there are reasons why men often hesitate to join grief support groups. Men are taught from an early age that expressing vulnerability, especially sadness or fear, is a sign of weakness. In the face of loss, they feel immense pressure to be the stoic protector and hold it together for family and friends. There is also a fear of judgment or stigma. Men may worry that showing deep emotion or admitting they need help will lead to them being perceived as less masculine by friends or peers. They may also feel that, as the minority, they would be outnumbered or unwelcome by women in the group.

This reluctance doesn't mean men don't grieve. They certainly do, but they may need a separate set of conditions to feel safe and comfortable. Of course our group is open to men and women. Everyone is welcome, and the space is one of comfort, acceptance, and confidentiality, where emotions like anger, sadness, or silence are accepted without judgment. The common goal is supporting each other in loss and focusing on the shared experience rather than gender.

When you lose a child and are looking for direction, you have three choices. You can either let that loss define you, let it destroy you, or let it strengthen you.

With collective support, many choose the path of resilience. Our group supports mothers who have risen in strength even when they didn't have any energy. That is the marvel of being associated with a bonded group of ladies who support and care for each other. We don't judge each other. We are each other's advocates, and we find strength in our numbers. We also never stop doing little things for others. Sometimes those small things occupy the biggest part of our hearts.

One thing I've learned is that grief does not end—it changes. Those who join grief support groups are not looking to erase their pain but to find ways to carry it. Through community, validation, and learning, they discover new ways to integrate loss into their lives. The group becomes a bridge between suffering and hope, a place where vulnerability is honored, and transformation is possible.

In the end, people choose grief support groups because they offer what the world often withholds: understanding, companionship, and the freedom to mourn without shame. In the quiet embrace of a circle, the bereaved find strength in each other, and loss, though still painful, becomes less lonely.

No one goes through grief alone. I encourage you to rely on family, friends, support groups, and those willing to listen.

Just listen.

Those who truly listen with a compassionate ear are a rare breed. When you find them, cherish them because they will strengthen you until you find the sun again.

I waited patiently for the LORD.
He turned to me and heard my cry.
He lifted me out of the pit of destruction,
out of the sticky mud.
He stood me on a rock
and made my feet steady.
—Psalm 40:1–2

31

A JOURNEY OF FAITH

Challenges are clouds that pass, revealing the sunshine of opportunity.
—Unknown

I remember attending vacation Bible school in the summers, singing in youth choirs, and attending youth group on Sunday nights. We took fun trips, and my church friends were my very best circle of friends. Mike and I attended church with our children, and they were involved in the angel choir and youth groups. They also made very good friends there, and church was a safe haven for us all.

We also participated in a Walk to Emmaus retreat, which was a Christian weekend for spiritual development and communing with friends. I did a lot of soul-searching about what was missing from my life. One of the speakers said, "If you are not going forward with your Christian walk, you are going backward. There is no standing still."

I realized that I was going backward, and I had developed a thirst for spiritual knowledge. Because of that moment, we formed a Bible study at my school that met each Friday before classes started. This group has continued to meet for over thirty years. We have supported each other through every kind of problem imaginable, from the death of children to the loss of spouses and parents, to health scares, to losing one of our members. The group has a beautiful silver scripture bracelet, and anytime someone was going through an exceptionally hard time, they were given the bracelet to wear and return when their hard journey was over.

This is the Scripture inscribed on the bracelet:

> ***"I say this because I know what I am planning for you," says the LORD. I have good plans for you, not plans to hurt you. I will give you hope and a good future.***
>
> **—Jeremiah 29:11**

How comforting these words are when you are hurting, to hear that God knows the big picture for all of us and will be there for us in the future. No matter what we must go through in life, good and bad, God is still in control. Even in difficult moments, we can have hope.

The bracelet was prayed over and given to anyone in our prayer group going through a difficult time. It was circulated among our group and became a source of remembrance that the group was praying for you during your hard time.

When Morgan died, my faithful Bible study friends met me at the hospital in Knoxville with open arms and outstretched hands, holding the silver bracelet ready to clasp around my wrist. With tears in my eyes, I accepted the bracelet, but I do remember saying, "This one is not coming back."

As I look back on my spiritual journey, delving into Bible study has made a big difference in the way I conduct my life and the way I raised my children. Kirk and Morgan saw me faithfully attend Friday morning Bible study throughout their childhoods, while their dad took them out for a special breakfast every week. Both Kirk and Morgan attended Chrysalis weekend, the youth version of Walk to Emmaus, and had good experiences with friends. Church gave my children the experience of Bible studies, and in high school, Young Life groups gave them opportunities to further their spiritual growth.

Morgan enjoyed her church group as well, and when she was about twelve years old, she went on a church trip to Nashville. The group was on Broadway, heading to a restaurant, when a group of young boys started a conversation. The youth counselor at the time teased that some of the boys were enamored with Morgan's long, blond hair and were following her group.

One of them, with admiring eyes, asked, "With your blond hair, are you Scandinavian?"

Morgan answered, "No, I'm Methodist."

Innocent enough, but there was no doubt that she loved her church and her church friends, even forming her identity around her deep faith.

Morgan's formal confirmation of faith in God and the church was at First Methodist. She was baptized as an infant at the altar of St. Andrew's Methodist Church in 1986, when she was four months old. I often think of all the activities and ministries in which Morgan and her youth group participated in over the years: retreats, Camp Lakeshore, Chrysalis, youth weeks, Young Life, and even conducting youth services. This was the place where Morgan's faith was formed and confirmed.

I know Morgan would not want us to mourn her death but rather celebrate her life. With her strong faith, I know I will see her shining face again in heaven. What a glorious day that will be!

Train children to live the right way,
and when they are old, they will not stray from it.
—Proverbs 22:6

I know I still have more growth to do in my faith, and I may face other faith crises in time. I also know that each one will be handled with prayer and with God leading the way.

32

NO GRIT, NO PEARL

All the sunsets are like shiny pearls strung together for a moment.
—Unknown

An irritant—a tiny grain of sand—can produce some of the most beautiful iridescent pearls in the world.

I was treated to a tour of Birdsong Resort, home of the Tennessee River Freshwater Pearl Farm, where I learned that pearls have been treasured since the thirteenth century. Long admired for their beauty, pearls were used in China for taxes, sewn on clothes in Persia, and in the Middle Ages were known as royal gems. Ancient writings associate pearls with weddings because they were too expensive for mass ownership.

Then, in 1896, Kokichi Mikimoto patented the process for culturing pearls. Since then, cultured pearls have become more affordable and available around the world.

Eight pilot farms conducted trials to culture pearls across the United States, but Birdsong Resort was the only one on the North American continent to successfully adapt the Japanese technique.

The founder of the Tennessee River Freshwater Pearl Farm, John Latendresse, married a Japanese woman and brought the custom over to America. They landed in Tennessee, where their first harvest of freshwater pearls was cultivated in 1984.

This farm is nestled in the pristine waters of Birdsong Creek. The cultivation process takes six months to four years, and today, Tennessee River pearls are among the most beautiful and durable in the world. The American Pearl Company collects and crafts the pearls into rings, necklaces, and earrings for gem-quality jewelry.

Today, Tennessee exports pearls to Japan and Tahiti because of the clean water conditions in which they are harvested.

Like the miracle of nature spinning sand into pearls, God can send us "pearls" during our moments of sorrow. One of my pearls appeared one week after Morgan's passing. My good friend Lynn, who had also lost a daughter, gave me a book that helped me during my first year of loss. While long out of print, it contained 365 days of comfort, each entry saying just what I needed that day. The authors of the book had lost two children, so they shared their wisdom and experience with others who had become separated from their loved ones.

That pearl of a book guided me week by week through the grieving process. I treasure it today and have given many copies to friends who have lost a child. My pearl that day was the book, and the grit in my life was the grief that pierced my heart. I learned to experience God's grace one day at a time. I could not have done it alone.

He has many other pearls for us. We just need to look for them.

Also, the kingdom of heaven is like a man looking for fine pearls. When he found a very valuable pearl, he went and sold everything he had and bought it.

—Matthew 13:45–46

There were many acts that honored Morgan's memory during the first weeks and months after her passing. Our nephew John had pink rubber bracelets made with her name on them for people to wear in remembrance of her. He passed them out to family and friends, and it was a tremendous act of support for our family. We received them in the first few weeks and still wear them in memory of Morgan.

Our twelve-year-old nephew, John, created a lasting memorial in that pink bracelet.

A pink bracelet.

A symbol of remembrance.

A symbol of her joy.

A symbol of her spirit living on in the memory of others.

Eleven years after Morgan was gone, I received this unexpected letter in the mail.

> September 11, 2017
>
> Mr. and Mrs. Mike McCarty,
>
> There are not many, any, in all honesty, days that go by where you and your family aren't in my thoughts. Morgan's pink wrist-band bracelet is still in my patrol car, and she's my driving force when I work crashes. I hope you are doing well and know that you're in my thoughts and prayers always.
>
> You're in my thoughts,
> Travis Shuler
> Knoxville Police Department

I remember that police officer as a comforting face in the sea of chaos at the hospital in Knoxville. So many years later, he still has Morgan's pink bracelet in his police car as he responds to crashes and helps people in danger.

His reassuring promise, "We will find the person who did this to Morgan," is as clear as the day he said it to Mike and me in the hospital. I had all the confidence in the world that he was telling the truth. It was like a warm blanket being wrapped around me, and I was comforted by his words and sincerity.

Due to the diligence of the Knoxville Police Department and Officer Travis Shuler, the driver was found. Travis had kept his word, and the driver was arrested six days after the accident.

What a gracious act of comfort from someone whose life touched ours so deeply eleven years earlier. He probably has no idea how much his letter meant to us and how it brought tears and smiles to our faces.

Travis, we appreciated you years ago as we faced the worst tragedy of our lives, and we appreciate your kindness now in reaching out to support parents who still miss their daughter.

Pearls like this will appear in your life.

My pearls came as a book on grief, a pink rubber bracelet, and a heartfelt letter written by a police officer. You never know what your pearls will be or when they will come. Whether they arrive immediately, like the book of comfort and the pink bracelets, or years later, like the letter, they will surprise you with grace, appearing in the most unlikely moments.

As you struggle through life's grit, I encourage you to always look for the pearls too. God's grace places them just where you need them.

33

MOVING ON

In three words I can sum up everything I've learned about life: it goes on.
—Robert Frost

After the loss of a loved one, we may lack the motivation to keep going. It can be tempting to quit trying, to sink into despair and assume our best days are behind us. But eventually, we have to find a way to move forward, even when it's hard.

There are many ways to acknowledge your feelings of grief. Sometimes we may lash out in ways that aren't helpful, or that may hurt the people we love. It's important to find positive outlets for our pain as we learn this new way of life. By expressing our emotions in honest and healthy ways, we can stop wallowing in the heavy emotions that threaten to sink us. It won't be easy, but I've discovered a few activities that can help us move forward on the other side of painful loss.

I have worked through many of these activities, some individually and others in group settings. Some you can do over and over again, while others may be completed just one time. Adjust what works for you as you are healing.

1. **Get active.** Walk outdoors, go to a park, or enjoy nature. Being around nature will create a positive mood. During bad weather, consider going to a gym or community center to walk or exercise indoors. Staying active is especially helpful when all you really want to do is hide away from the world.
2. **Plant a special place in your loved one's memory.** Consider planting a memory garden, adding mementos or flowers that they loved, or acknowledging them with a stone or symbol that represents their favorite things. I always plant pink tulips and pink zinnias in the summer and fresh pansies in the winter on Morgan's grave. When I visit, I can walk around the cemetery to see the treasures that have been lovingly placed near the headstones by their loved ones. I've seen everything from college banners to Mardi Gras beads to teddy bears and plush toys. Each token has been placed there with love, and each act has surely helped a grieving visitor feel connected to their loved one.
3. **Tell your story.** It feels good to write down your thoughts as you journey through grief. Take a moment to write your way through it, especially on hard days like birthdays. These writings do not have to be shared. Write freely, knowing no one will ever read them. Release all those emotions from your body and share all the things you don't always say aloud. You can even burn or shred the entry once it is written but allow yourself this time to write about every worry, fear, resentment, question, and emotion flowing through you. If you have faith, let this serve as a conversation between you and God, trusting that anything you say is already known and understood, and that every human emotion you're expressing is acceptable and allowed.
4. **Be still.** I love opening the door to my screened porch in the early mornings and listening to the birds as they wake up the neighborhood. It gives me hope for the new day ahead. Put on the kettle or brew coffee and meditate or pray in the stillness of your home. I like to get up first thing in the morning while the house is quiet. With no distractions, I use

this time to connect spiritually with God and with Morgan, while steadying my soul and preparing for the day ahead.

5. **Take personal time.** Light candles and take a bubble bath. Have your hair styled, get a manicure, splurge on a massage or facial, or take time to pamper yourself with your favorite activities. These little gifts for your soul will result in an aromatic lifting of your spirit.
6. **Remember the good.** Create a list of the personality traits that best describe your child. I keep a list in my journal and revisit it every so often, usually with a smile. I often remind myself that the painful end of Morgan's life was just one devastating moment. We still have more than two decades of happy memories and moments to celebrate. She was so vibrant, personable, and full of life. I choose to focus on all the *life* she brought to our world, rather than the loss we all felt when she was taken too soon. That perspective helps me stay positive and grateful rather than sinking into bitterness.
7. **Be creative.** Paint, draw, design, and use your talents to express yourself. Want to try a new skill or hobby? Take a class. It's never too late to learn. My grandmother Kirk started oil painting and writing poetry at seventy-five. We can overcome our negative emotions by creating something positive and beautiful in their place.
8. **Escape.** Watch a movie and enjoy your comfort foods. Chocolate cake for supper? Yes!
9. **Read for pleasure.** As tempting as it is to always be productive, I encourage you to step away from the self-improvement titles for a while and read something just for fun. Escape into a lighthearted romance novel or join a book club and enjoy discussing stories with your friends. Reading can offer a peaceful escape when reality becomes too much to bear. And with public libraries offering so many wonderful titles, you don't have to spend a penny for a dose of feel-good literature.
10. **Lift others up.** Share the gift of time with others. Take a meal to someone who is struggling. Maybe you have an

elderly neighbor who is feeling lonely, a friend battling an illness, or a community member suffering their own loss. Drive someone to the store or to a doctor's appointment, or just take a friend to lunch. Find ways to enjoy the company of others.

Trust the Lord with all your heart,
and don't depend on your understanding.
Remember the Lord in all you do,
and he will give you success.
—Proverbs 3:5–6

Another way to honor your loved one's memory is to reconstruct their life in a scrapbook. Through tissues and tears, it can become a comforting heirloom to cherish once you're finished.

I compiled volumes of photo albums and scrapbooks, documenting both of our children's lives. They were organized by year and include all the sports albums with news clippings, programs, and any other important material that helped capture the many special memories our family shared.

But then, out of nowhere, raging water overflowed a nearby creek and rushed into our basement. It was called the five-hundred-year flood, and it caught us completely off guard.

I asked my friend Charlie, who owned a frame shop, for advice. I wanted to preserve the soggy photos, but I didn't know what to do.

"Most of what was damaged can be easily replaced except for our precious pictures," I explained. "The photos are irreplaceable. The albums were all drenched."

"Get the pictures out of the albums and dry them flat with wax paper between each photo," Charlie instructed. "It might take a while, but the photos need to be separated from the wet albums so they can dry."

What a task! With thirty or more albums, we had thousands of pictures to save. We had almost nowhere to step because of all the pictures drying on the floors. We spread the word, and our friends came and took albums, letting the photos dry out at their homes. We had pictures drying all over our town. I was thankful that the pictures did dry out, as Charlie said they would. The scrapbooks and all the memorabilia were returned dry and safe.

I felt tremendous appreciation for all the friends who'd helped save our pictures. Now I had to face the big job ahead—reorganizing all the photos.

Thankfully, we saved hundreds of adorable baby pictures of my children; all their school pictures; pictures representing every holiday, showcasing our Easter dresses, Halloween costumes, and Christmas finery; pictures of birthdays; and vacation pictures that let us relive the fun through all of Morgan's ages. Finding her cheerleading pictures from age seven up to high school, seeing the uniforms she wore so proudly, as well as the competition dance team pictures and their awards, helped me relive those happy times with pride in all she had done.

As long as it takes, I will lovingly labor to put together the timeless souvenirs of our life together. I cling to the photo books, for they hold my forever memories. If you don't think photos are important, wait until they are all you have left.

I thank my God every time I remember you, always praying with joy for all of you.
—Philippians 1:3–4

34

EIGHT THINGS I NOW UNDERSTAND

A sunny disposition is worth more than fortune.
—Andrew Carnegie

When I wasn't teaching, I discovered that time can be hard to fill, and an unoccupied mind is not a good thing following a terrible tragedy. Finding a part-time job, volunteering in your community or church, or taking up a hobby can be effective ways to stay engaged.

I noticed a shared interest in reading at my church, so I started a book club with a group of friends. Organizing and selecting books took time and helped me focus on others rather than myself. Thirteen years later, our group hosts guest authors and embarks on out-of-town field trips to literary sites, and our numbers keep growing. I still look forward to gathering each month for our group discussions.

Gardening is another hobby I enjoy. Our local UT Extension office offers an outstanding Master Gardener Program, which I joined a few years ago. With its year-round projects, I can stay busy every month of the year with the opportunities that are available.

Our community also offers opportunities to tutor second graders in our local schools. My husband, who had never worked with children in a school setting, told me, "I feel led to volunteer." I reminded him about his inexperience with school-age children and his impatience. I didn't recommend it. Despite my concerns, he persisted and signed up.

Much to my surprise, he enjoyed working with seven-year-olds and was rewarded for his efforts with adoring students who looked forward to his weekly visit. They ended up being the highlight of his week. He has not only demonstrated great patience with the kids, but he has also built a real rapport and a strong connection with them too.

Mike also got involved in our church, teaching and leading a small group. This kept him busy preparing and studying for upcoming lessons. Communities offer so many avenues to keep you working and learning. Reach out and try something new.

Finding fresh and meaningful rituals can bring purpose to your life and help you survive. It might even change your life and save it at the same time.

EIGHT REALITIES OF CHILD LOSS

1. **You will grieve for a lifetime.** Each person should be allowed to grieve in his or her own way and time. Some prefer the company of others, while others need space to be alone. Grief will never fully leave, but it should change as the healing journey progresses and we move through grief's various stages.
2. **The date may define your life.** The day we lose our child will forever divide our lives with a before-and-after mark. From that moment on, everything will be remembered as happening either before or after the date.
3. **Faith can be your rock.** My faith carried me when I could not carry myself. Whether you find strength in a higher power, the enduring laws of nature, or the resilience of the human spirit, there is a universal foundation to lean on.
4. **No one grieves alone.** Remember that you are not alone in your pain. While no one will grieve to the same degree as a parent, grandparents, siblings, cousins, aunts, uncles, and friends are also devastated. By allowing them to take care of

you, you're also helping them process their own grief and giving them the opportunity to heal through service.

5. **Triggers come unexpectedly.** Someone may casually ask if you have any children. A song may suddenly play that your child enjoyed. You may come across a forgotten memento or drive past a special location that draws a memory to the surface. It's okay to let these unexpected emotions rise when needed.
6. **Special days are hard.** Holidays may be too sad without your child. During the first year, especially, you may need to break with old traditions and allow for new ones to take shape.
7. **Talk about your child with others.** Saying your child's name and sharing stories will keep their memory alive.
8. **Share with families who have been through the loss of a child.** They are usually the only ones who can possibly understand what you are going through. They can become a real source of strength and support as you heal.

Everyone's grief looks different. Just because someone carries it well doesn't mean it isn't heavy. People may look one way on the outside while feeling turmoil and pain on the inside. I encourage you to be sensitive as you gently approach people experiencing the tender season of grief.

But the people who trust the Lord will become strong again.
They will rise up as an eagle in the sky;
they will run and not need rest;
they will walk and not become tired.
—Isaiah 40:31

35

MILESTONES

A sunset never truly leaves.
Its warmth and light remain in our memories and hearts forever.
—Unknown

Certain milestones prepare a child for life's journey as they grow toward independence. One of the first times a mother faces separation is when her child starts kindergarten. I was fortunate that Kirk and Morgan were able to attend the school where I taught. In fact, they were both able to attend that same campus with me all the way through the fifth grade, so their first day of sixth grade felt more like their first day of kindergarten to me.

Once they reached sixth grade, they were probably delighted to be out from under Mom's watchful eye, but this arrangement proved to be quite an adjustment for me. It was the first time they were inaccessible to me during the day.

I had grown accustomed to them popping into my classroom to get a paper signed or money for lunch, a book fair, a field trip, or something they'd forgotten. Now I wouldn't be there to help.

The transition went smoothly with Kirk since I still had three more years with Morgan. It was harder when Morgan advanced, and I was the only one left at the elementary school.

That was the first milestone in their move toward independence. I had always told my husband, "Kiss them goodbye when they get their driver's license," and that proved to be true.

The next milestone of their independence occurred with the long-awaited driver's license. The day each of my children turned sixteen, it was off to the DMV for the test. Neither could wait to drive.

Kirk's first solo drive was to a high school bonfire and pep rally at school. After going over all the rules, he assured us, with confidence and excitement, "Mom, I'll be careful and will be home as soon as it is over."

I was happy for him, but I held back tears, feeling pride and concern.

Mike tried to ease my worries. "Pam, Kirk has been driving since he was thirteen years old with your dad's old Jeep on the farm. He's more than ready to head out on his own."

Together, Mike and I stood in the driveway, waving like he was going to another country. Pacing the floor and looking at the clock, I was nervous until he pulled in the driveway in one piece. Mike teased that he was glad the car was in one piece.

Our son's independence had begun. Little did I know my worry was just beginning. Kirk has been driving for more than twenty-five years now, but my concerns for his safety remain just as strong today.

A mother's heart never rests.

With a December birthday, Morgan was one of the first in her class to drive. She was excited not to be carted around by her big brother anymore. She had found double independence—from both Kirk and me.

I was still apprehensive about her going out on her own, but I learned to enjoy my new freedom from not having to drive her to and from dance and cheer practice each week. There were real advantages, but it took me a long time to discover them.

A much harder tug at the heartstrings occurred when the kids went away to college.

First, Kirk headed off to UT. I was emotional but kept it together, focusing on the practical business of packing and getting his clothes ready for the big move. I somehow held back the tears throughout the four-and-a-half-hour drive to campus. But the floodgates opened when we drove out of Kirk's sight. I cried all the way home.

Once again, steady Mike tried to reason with me. "Pam, he'll be home in a month or so."

But I kept worrying about all the struggles he'd face without me there to help him. "Does he have enough clothes? What about spending money? It's such a big campus. Will he find all his classes?"

All these fears were driving me crazy.

Again, Mike reminded me, "He has a cell phone with him, and I can get him if I need to anytime. Let's give him a little space and time. He will call when he gets settled into the dorm."

As parents, our goal is to send our children off into the world as healthy young adults. Gaining their independence when going off to college is a proud moment, but nobody warns us about how hard it will be for the parents.

"I finally realized that if my children are happy in their new surroundings, then Mama is happy," I told my sister.

And Kirk was happy.

I was surprised when my introverted son joined a fraternity and was thrilled to be on the Knoxville campus. The fact that he was becoming involved in college life was music to my ears, but I still clung to those brief holidays or quick visits for the UT football games, where we got to visit and catch up with him.

Morgan, our extrovert, jumped with both feet into college life and never looked back.

The day she moved into her dorm at UT, her roommate had not yet arrived, and she wanted to set up her room right away. She didn't really want much help. She chose to tackle it by herself and get all her stuff organized just the way she wanted. Mike and I left her in her room since she did not want to wait until the next day to get settled into the dorm.

"That night was hard," I told my sister. "We left and went to eat with promises of seeing her for lunch the next day. That was when it really sank in that she was going to be gone."

Mike knew what was coming when I started crying at the restaurant. "Pam, you're going to see her tomorrow."

"I know, but this means she is on her own," I tried to explain. "I felt the same way when Kirk left."

"And look how well you adjusted. It will be the same with Morgan. It's her turn."

"Yes, I agree, Mike. It is her turn, but it doesn't make it any easier," I said, wiping away my tears.

Then, two weeks after dropping Morgan off at UT for her freshman year, we received this letter from her in the mail:

9/9/04

Mom and Dad,

Thanks so much for the package of M&M brownies. They were good! Dad, your CDs are great that you burned for me. I'm bumping now to the new tunes! Ha Ha.

I miss y'all so much, and I can't wait to see y'all at homecoming. Y'all are the best parents ever! School is so much fun! No regrets on UTK!

Love and miss you lots,

Morgan

I smiled as I read her letter.

She's happy. She's content. She has no regrets. That's all a mother could ask for. While her new group of friends and her new sorority kept her happy and engaged in school, I spent most of my weekends sending costumes and outfits to her for mixers and dances.

A fifties dress? Sure, we've got that. An eighties formal? Yes, I can find that too.

Seeing your children content and doing what they love is all a parent can hope for.

Kirk's college experience was great, and Morgan's was great too—until it wasn't.

BETH MOORE, in her book *Feathers from My Nest*, describes her reaction to her children leaving home from the viewpoint of a pair of sparrows.

"What is what, my love?
What if they fly back home after we have raised them to climb the wind?"...
"But the little one, Mr. Sparrow. She was so young."...
"She is young, yes. But she is strong just like her sister. You'll see.
Fine sparrows they are, dear Mrs. Let them fly."
"As if I could have stopped them."

I could relate to the question of whether Kirk and Morgan were ready to leave the nest. That worry must go through every parent's mind. *Have I taught them enough? Are they ready?*

My sisters tell me that when I went away to college, our mother "just ceased cooking."

I doubt that really happened, but they did say she had a hard time adjusting. Now, I understand. We have them under our wings for eighteen years, and then, poof! They're gone.

Letting go is never easy, but it's necessary, even though it pulls at our heartstrings every time we have to say goodbye. These big milestones will happen, and I am grateful for the milestones I had with my two children. I learned to let them fly...as if I could have stopped them.

The Lord has told you, human, what is good;
he has told you what he wants from you:
to do what is right to other people,
love being kind to others,
and live humbly, obeying your God.
—Micah 6:8

36

GRIEF LESSONS

You will never finish being a daughter.
You will be one 'til the end of my days.
—Unknown

Margaret Mead has been attributed with saying, "When a person is born, we rejoice, and when they are married, we jubilate, but when they die, we try to pretend that nothing happened."

That is the attitude of many who prefer to skip the grieving process and go on as if nothing has happened. But when grief knocks on our door, it will keep knocking until we have no choice but to invite it in for a while.

When Morgan died, I wanted to fast-forward through the painful first year of grief and be healed. I wanted our world to go back to the way it was before she was taken from us, but that was impossible. The healing—and the acceptance—would have to follow their own timetable.

Some days, I thought I would never smile again. I feared all my days would be filled with excruciating pain, sorrow, and loss. While I'm sure I will always experience some painful days, I now find far more moments of peace and joy than of despair. But I couldn't have handled such a devastating loss by relying on my strength alone. The grief was bigger than anything I could manage, so I relied on God to get me through.

I know faith can be difficult, especially when you've lost a loved one and might even feel angry at God for allowing such a horrible thing to happen. Maybe you've never developed a spiritual foundation, or perhaps you lost your faith in the wake of grief. I'm not trying to tell you what to believe, but I can share that for me, faith is all that has gotten me through this journey. So I encourage you to consider finding a spiritual practice that feels right for you. As the Bible tells us, even a tiny mustard seed of faith can be enough.

Now that I look back through the years, I can understand the lessons I've learned from bearing the unbearable. I'm not the same person I was when Morgan was alive. The day she passed away will forever divide my life into Before and After. But now I can see the many ways this painful loss has shaped me.

Grief taught me to see the bereavement of others. I had lost grandparents, aunts, and uncles, but never anyone in my immediate family. After losing my child, I understood the grief of others in a way I had never understood before. I hurt as others hurt, and I could grieve along with them in their time of need. I remember a family on our street who lost a child when I was a young girl. I felt so sad for the family, but I never realized the heartache they were going through. Now I have a much better understanding of the depths of others' pain.

Grief taught me that I am not in control of what happens in my life. Death doesn't just happen to other people. I was an educator in control of my students and my family. In an instant, my world was turned upside down. I discovered instantly that I had no control. There is no way of knowing when your life will change. But at some point in time, something might bring you to your knees.

Grief taught me that tasks that once seemed so important now take a backseat. Things that once consumed my time seem unimportant now, such as fretting over what fabric to use for a chair or sofa, or having just the right outfit to wear to a party. Today, I see the effort that went into meaningless priorities. I love to have an orderly house and a new outfit for a special occasion, but I no longer focus on such superficial worries. I've learned that I wear the same five or six items of clothing repeatedly. My house is more than comfortable. I don't need new things to impress anyone. Grief helps prioritize your life in the best way.

Grief taught me to appreciate the simple moments. When someone you love dies, you no longer feel joy when the holidays, birthdays, promotions, and vacations arrive. What used to be a special cause for celebration doesn't bring the same excitement. Instead, it's the normal, everyday moments we ache for most. I still long for a phone call just to hear Morgan's voice. I yearn for the tropical-flower smell of her luxurious hair. I pine to hear her car pull up in the driveway. Those seemingly trivial moments really are what matter most.

Grief taught me that I will never again be the person I was before Morgan died. Life has changed, and I have also changed. My challenge is learning how to cope without the physical presence of my daughter. I try to think of Morgan and how she would have wanted me to live. I wake up every day and aim to be productive and happy. For whatever reason, I am here, and she is not, so I choose to continue with my life in a way that would please her and make her proud.

Grief taught me that I had to give myself permission to grieve. It's a conscious choice to move through the process of grief and heal. I learned to honor that process and take as much time as needed to restore my life.

Grief taught me the importance of rest. The body, soul, and mind need quiet space and time to recover. Nature understands this. Just as a butterfly knows when to take shelter from a storm, we too know when to take cover. We can fly again once the storm has passed. What we can't do is dodge grief. That would be a bit like trying to tiptoe around the rain.

Grief taught me that deep mourning is a lot like a roller coaster. Some days, we will be up and feeling better, and other days, we might be in tears at the bottom again. It's okay to feel the ups and downs. Even when we hit smoother seasons, we may be caught off guard by certain moments, anniversaries, places, songs, or smells. They will drop us back into the well of pain, but we can hold on to hope, knowing that we won't stay down forever.

Grief taught me that everyone grieves at their own pace and in their own way. There is no one true path toward healing, and a deep loss is not something to get over quickly. Well-meaning people may say you need closure. That word doesn't sit right with me. Bank accounts close; windows close; doors close; roads close; but the love we have for our loved ones will never close. Why? Because there is no end to the grief journey. It's just a new reality we must learn to navigate in the best way possible—one day at a time.

Are you familiar with the children's game, *Going on a Bear Hunt*? My granddaughters love to play it, and when I hear them singing the familiar rhyme, their words remind me of the grief journey many of us are going through.

> You can't go around it,
> You can't get over it,
> You can't go under it,
> You have to go through it.

Just like a bear hunt, grief gives us no shortcuts. It's a response to the deep love we carry for our loved one, and that's no easy load to carry.

While no one wants to become a bereaved parent, this journey has brought many amazing people into my life. Bereaved parents share a special and common bond of understanding that lasts a lifetime. The connection with others who grieve is strong and emotional.

Everyone grieves, but not everyone heals. By giving yourself time to replace negative thoughts with positive ones, you can begin moving toward peace of mind. Just as a flower needs water to bloom, we need moments of respite to rest, recharge, and thrive. So take a deep breath, put your worries on hold, and give yourself a gift of pause. It's not a sign of weakness, but rather a necessity for strength. Let your mind and body unwind, and you'll be amazed at how much better you can tackle life's challenges—even in the wake of grief.

37

EXISTING IN JOY

I will live in the sunshine of your life, instead of the darkness of your death.
—Unknown

I was blessed to have had twenty wonderful years with my daughter, Morgan Leah McCarty. Do I wish I had more? Certainly. I cherish the precious time I had with her and would have wanted it to go on forever. But the bond I formed with Morgan cannot be broken, not even by death.

I still miss the sound of her voice and the stories she shared.

I miss the playfulness of her laughter and her love of fashion.

I miss her eyes full of expectation and wonder.

But I will live with her love alive in my heart, and the memories will last forever.

Each day, I try to be a "little more like Morgan"—more kind, more loving, more giving, more fun. The peace that passes all understanding enables me to remember her with joy and smiles instead of dwelling on the heartache, loss, and tears.

I've learned that it's up to me to see the love that remains and to celebrate it every day.

I've found that, little by little, grieving parents can find joy again.

Of course, the transition isn't easy. And it takes time.

Yes, the scars will remain tender for as long as we live. The pain won't ever completely heal.

But that jagged wound of grief won't always be the fresh, deep hurt it was at first. With faith and hope, it will transform into a constant reminder that we have survived unbearable trauma and are still here, living one day at a time in memory and in honor of the child we loved and lost. I know it may seem impossible to envision a future without your beloved child. But let me encourage you to get up every morning, take a deep breath, and start the day without your child in it.

Morgan's chair at the dinner table is permanently empty. Her vacant room is hard to glance into when I pass by. Her high school picture is still in view. All of this brings a flood of happy and sad memories, sometimes threatening to sink me again.

But I thank God for the occasional night when I see her in my dreams. Usually, she appears as a young child, playing happily, as she did when she was growing up. After those dreams, I always wake up smiling, grateful to have had such a beautiful vision and visit, knowing that even death cannot keep her from me. Though I will grieve the death of my daughter forever, my life is not lacking in joy and happiness. Just the opposite, though I admit it took a long time to get there.

Today, my life is exuberantly rich again, as it was before Morgan's tragic death. I live from a deeper place now, and I love more deeply still. Because I have experienced such immeasurable grief, I have come to know joy like no other. After dragging myself back from the pit of pure hell and overcoming such intense pain and sorrow, I find that when joy comes now, it explodes with a new meaning and thankfulness.

You too can learn to celebrate each positive moment in your life with robust gusto, taking nothing for granted. Knowing the sacred preciousness of life gives me more of a reason to be thankful for what I have every single day.

Two of my greatest pleasures today are my granddaughters. What fun and wonder I find in watching them grow. Every moment with them transports me to a state of bliss. Grandchildren are truly a blessing, and their sweet laughter gives me hope for the future. Thankfully, I have the privilege of being an active part of their lives. My son Kirk and his family give me joy each time I visit, and I am grateful to him for sharing their lives with me. I love and appreciate them daily and savor every second we can be together.

I realize that not everyone has the gift of other children or grandchildren, but I encourage you to seek the joys and blessings in your life. Embrace friends and family and enjoy their company and companionship.

It's my hope that you can continually find reasons to share memories of your loved one. Remember, you are the keeper of the footprint of their life. Record each picture, treasure each random moment, and keep an inventory of their life. Look at photos, write about your loved one, say their name, and hold it close. Always be open to stories and memories that others share with you. Laugh and love with those who knew their smile and the way their eyes twinkled with delight.

"There is nothing I love more than hearing a story, whether it's one I haven't heard about Morgan or one that I have heard hundreds of times. It never gets old," I shared with my Grace for Grief Group.

Did your child love fishing? Hiking? Music? Or game nights? Maybe they enjoyed going to concerts, sporting events, or theater productions. Whatever made them happy, I encourage you to engage in those activities and find deep connection with your loved one again.

Make choices in your life that honor your child. Make them proud of your decisions as you choose to live in a way that helps others and honors their memory. Take an emotional risk. Take chances and say what you feel, hold back nothing, and dance as if no one is watching. Listen to music your child enjoyed. Sing at the top of your lungs.

As mentioned earlier, we established a scholarship foundation in Morgan's name, and we host a golf classic every year to help students fund their college education. But you don't have to plan grand gestures to honor your child. I also honor Morgan in simple ways, such as wearing pink because she loved that color. By wearing pink, I have a feel-good connection to her.

Every time I pull out my grandmother's beautiful crystal-glass salad dish to use, it brings a smile to my face and warm memories of eating Sunday lunches at her house with her fabulous fruit salad.

Recreating my mother's recipes is comforting and brings me closer to her. Nothing reminds me more of growing up at home than my mother's creamed eggs on toast for breakfast. They were such a treat.

Wearing my straw hats in the summer and my felt hats in the winter reminds me of how my father wore his broad-brimmed Stetson cowboy hat all the time.

My sweet aunt Peggy made me a stained-glass butterfly that hangs in my office window. Seeing the light shining brightly through the glass reminds me of her funny laugh, and it makes me smile.

The pink clothes, dishes, recipes, butterfly, and all the hats are little reminders of the love I have for each one of these special people in my life. These simple moments help create an environment of thankfulness for our loved ones. They remind us of how fortunate we were to know them and give us a chance to keep their memories alive with us each day.

I also encourage you to gather strength from others. We are not alone in our journey.

Let us, then, feel very sure that we can come before
God's throne where there is grace. There we can receive mercy and
grace to help us when we need it.
—Hebrews 4:16

38

CHANNELING YOUR LIGHT

Hope is being able to see that there is light despite all of the darkness.
—Desmond Tutu

Grief takes over our lives. After the loss of a child, we are different people and will never be the same again. The process of change is painful and difficult, yet when we come through the other side, we can find hope and joy.

Your journey is not yours alone. Many people are going through the same pain and heartache. Reaching out is a natural way to share your experiences with others, helping them feel less alone. Sharing your light is the next step.

You should teach people whom you can trust the things you and many others have heard me say. Then they will be able to teach others.
—2 Timothy 2:2

Mentors are trusted guides who have navigated the difficult terrain to the top of the mountain and have survived the climb back down. They then offer to lead others on the best path. Along the trail, you'll face pitfalls and boulders that will cause you to detour. Being warned of hazards ahead will help you avoid mistakes and keep your pathway smoother.

A guide can give you confidence and encouragement to help you make it to the end of the journey. As steep and hard as the path may be, the reward is waiting at the end of the climb.

At first, you'll be the one in need of a teacher. Pride can make us want to tackle the journey solo. Pain can make us want to isolate and push people away. But those choices only make our journey harder than it needs to be. Trusting those who have walked ahead of us in this grief can be lifesaving, healing, and helpful.

Once you've learned your mentor's ways, you can reach out and become that guide for others during their deepest seasons of grief. You can use your new knowledge to lead them through the steps you've been taking during your own grief journey.

Some may feel unqualified to help anyone, just as I did when I felt called to start our Grace for Grief group. But look at all you've already overcome. It was not easy at first, and you may have relied on others to help you take those first steps, whether a minister, a friend, a loved one, a medical professional, a counselor, or a funeral director. We all need guidance through these turbulent times, as this is not something we ever expect to face. No one can be prepared to bury their child, so we not only want guidance, we need it. Especially from another parent who has navigated that grief.

But once you reach the top of your mountain, you can begin to see the bigger view. You realize that your life will not always feel so dark and hopeless. While the pain will never end, you can learn to live with hope in your heart again. You can make room for both sorrow and joy, darkness and light, loss and love.

That's why I encourage you to find a mentor and then, at the right time, become one yourself. While many people feel uncomfortable stepping into the mentor role, especially if they've never been a teacher, counselor, or leader, you don't need any special training to help someone. Start small. Can you go to someone who is hurting and just be with them and listen? Can you show care by running errands, bringing groceries, or cooking a meal? It may mean making a phone call just to say, "I am here for you." Maybe you can send a note or card to cheer someone up, or give a hug when others are at their lowest point.

My secret weapon to help you move forward is grace. Grace is what enables us to use gifts that are free and undeserved. We access grace like every other spiritual tool, by asking for it specifically and regularly.

Grace reaches where you are and takes you where God wants you to be. It has the power to do something that nothing else can do—transform your heart. God's grace intervenes to give us power and strength. It gives us the ability to not only do what we're called to do, but also what we could never do on our own.

Reaching out to others offers reassurance. By lending a sympathetic ear, without judgment, you can confirm the wide range of emotions a person experiences. Since you've been through deep grief, you can offer assurance that the person is not alone and that they can make it through the worst moments of their loss.

Think of the people who have influenced you. Are you willing to reach out to others? Rejoice with them as they move out of the darkness and into the light.

You are the light that gives light to the world.... In the same way, you should be a light for other people. Live so that they will see the good things you do and will praise your Father in heaven.
—Matthew 5:14, 16

Your journey through grief has led you this far. Now you can serve as a source of hope and a guiding light for the living. Embrace life and be the beacon to guide others to Christ.

I do not pretend to understand the unfairness of life. God's love is not dependent on how you look, how you act, or how perfect a life you have led. No matter your story, God understands. His love is non-negotiable.

I have experienced a faithful God, and I know, firsthand, that I could not have made it through this loss without my faith. So, I encourage you to do as I do. Run to Jesus. Jesus wants you to come to him. His word is like a balm for our anxious hearts.

We will all face pain, heartache, and struggles here on earth. But our faith assures us there is no need to get stuck in despair. Those who have left us have no pain, heartache, or struggles. They are in the safe, loving arms of Jesus. Those arms are the best place to be. We do not have to worry.

Our children are, at this moment, at peace in the presence of God. Think about that. What more could a parent ask for? That is the goal for all of us.

Remember, while we've lost a loved one, others remain here in our lives today. We can't allow ourselves to miss out on the moments here with the living. As we've learned, we never know when a life will be stolen from us. Whether we have a short or long season with those who remain, we must treasure that time because there are no guarantees of days or hours spent in our loved one's presence.

I have learned to be filled with gladness for the time I'm given with loved ones. And I'm grateful for the time I had with my daughter, Morgan. I was blessed with so many wonderful years as her mother, and that's a gift I will never take for granted.

We can choose to be joyful and celebrate the life of our child even after they are gone.

Despite my initial objection and instincts, I quickly came around to my daughter's wishes about organ donation. We learned that, in 2025, more than forty thousand organ transplants were performed in the US because of the generosity of donors. One donor has the power to save and extend up to eight lives. More than one hundred thousand people are waiting for an organ transplant in the US today.

Due to the shortage of available organs, thirteen people die each day waiting for an organ transplant. To become an organ donor, you can register with the National Donate Life Registry, your state registry site, or your local DMV or BMV, depending on your state. Your choice can be noted on your state driver's license or ID.

I encourage you to let your family know your desire, so your wishes can be followed. This can be a lifesaving gift for others.

At the hospital on the day my daughter died, four people received lifesaving organs from Morgan. What a gift of life, but what a price for us to pay. A bittersweet act for our family, it was a precious second chance for others:

- Her right lung went to someone in Ohio.
- One kidney, to someone in Nashville.
- The other kidney, to someone in Texas.
- Her liver, to a forty-eight-year-old mother in Memphis.

My wise son, Kirk, stepped up to inform us that organ donation was Morgan's wish. Morgan's light will live on because, by donating her organs, she was even generous in death. Morgan has taught us in so many ways to be the light for others.

Morgan's Aunt Denise honored Morgan in a special, meaningful way too. "One way I could channel my grief," she said, "was to donate to an organ donor organization by buying a Florida license plate in memory of Morgan. The idea of using MLMLO on an organ donor plate came to me as a valid statement of how I felt."

Morgan Leah McCarty Lives On

MLMLO

Her light still shines.

I leave you my peace; my peace I give you. I do not give it to you as the world does. So don't let your heart be troubled or afraid.

—John 14:27

Morgan in her modeling days

A UT college visit

The McCarty family on vacation in Destin, Florida

Morgan in Destin with her rainbow in the background

Morgan's senior picture

Morgan in her apartment at UT

Morgan and her brother, Kirk, as young kids

Morgan and her dad, Mike

Morgan at age three

ACKNOWLEDGMENTS

The completion of this book has been a labor of love and made possible through the invaluable support of family and friends. To Mike, the love of my life, I extend my deepest gratitude for your unwavering patience and encouragement during the long days and months of writing. You helped me give Morgan a voice while encouraging and supporting me from start to finish.

To Kirk, my son, who was my sounding board for family stories throughout my children's childhood years. You have been my support from the very beginning of my writing adventure. Thank you for helping me find my voice and being the finest chapter of my life.

To my sisters, Donna and Kandy, who provided insightful feedback and contributed to the experiences that shaped both of my children's narratives. This book is as much a testament to your support as it is to my journey. I couldn't have walked this path without you.

To Denise, they say you don't choose your family, but if I could, I'd choose you every time. Thank you for being my confidant and for making the heavy parts of this journey a little lighter. And to Deborah, having your support meant the world to me.

This story formed in my mind long before I wrote the first word. I knew I wanted to write the story of my journey with Morgan, but I lacked a dedicated block of time to give it the attention it needed. Enter Julie Cantrell with an email about a Story Summit master class that she would be teaching on writing a memoir. With the guidance of Debra Engle and Julie, and in collaboration with an inspiring writing group, I was able to progress from a concept to a complete manuscript. Their expertise and encouragement have been invaluable throughout this endeavor.

I would also like to acknowledge the members of my Story Summit "Story Squad," who reviewed every line and laughed and cried their way through my entire book, one chapter at a time. A simple thank-you is not enough. Your support, encouragement, and camaraderie kept me going until the end.

To Bridget Beck, our sunflower farm girl and champion of social justice; to Julie Klein, Juliebird, who was brave enough to share her vulnerable memoir; to Cat Wyatt, our adventurous Alaskan spirit; and Sarah Mathews, our attorney and dancing queen, you have been my rock stars throughout this entire process. Finally, to our fearless group leader, Julie Cantrell, who possesses the ability to elevate the work of everyone around her, your commitment and empathy helped bring Morgan's story to life.

I am grateful for my beta readers who waded through my first draft and contributed my first set of critiques—Joy Austin, Torre Kelley, Becky Lane, Elizabeth Johnson, Linda Page, Sarah Mathews, and Maggie Rheney. I am thankful for their constructive critiques and recommendations, which were essential in refining the initial draft.

My wonderful Grace for Grief group provided ongoing encouragement and valuable perspectives drawn from personal experience. You were my research base. You helped with many parts of the book, because you have lived it with your own children. Thanks to Judy, Patsy, Sherry, Becky, Martha, Jan, Torre, Robin, and to our Norma, your support has meant so much.

Tremendous thanks to Morgan's close friends, who shared their stories, letters, and tributes that spanned her years from elementary age to college. Karen, Katey, Robyn, Rachael, Kara, Megan, UT Kappa Kappa Gamma friends, Jenn Hendrick, Ashley Gilley, and others who contributed a lifetime of fun and friendship, thanks so much. These memories are deeply appreciated. I love each and every one of you!

To The Morgan Leah McCarty Memorial Scholarship Foundation board of directors, I am so blessed to have such a talented group of friends who helped establish this foundation and have kept it going for twenty years. To date, we have raised half a million dollars for scholarships because of your hard work and efforts. I am a lucky person to have such valued friends.

I am thankful to Senator Don McLeary, Senator Lowe Finney, and Representative Jimmy Eldridge for their efforts in introducing the McCarty-Britt Bill in the Tennessee state legislature.

I appreciate all the representatives and senators from both sides of the House who backed our bill. Big thanks to Representative Eldridge, who sponsored the bill and carried it across the finish line to pass after many weeks and months of calls, emails, and appearances at the Capitol. Also, thanks to Tom Britt, who supported the efforts and helped with the local press and television news.

To Ember & Vine Press under the guidance of Julie Cantrell and Janyre Tromp. With your experience, I knew I would be in good hands placing my memoir with your group. Your commitment to excellence is evident in everything you do. I express my sincere gratitude for the work making this book come true for me.

Finally, I would like to acknowledge Morgan, whose life served as the inspiration for this work. It has been a privilege to share her story of positivity and kindness. In writing this book, I aimed to accomplish two primary goals. First, to introduce readers to Morgan and allow them to become acquainted with the daughter I cherished, highlighting her engaging and compassionate personality. Second, I sought to provide support to families coping with loss by sharing my personal experiences with grief. My intention is for this book to offer insight, comfort, grace, and peace to others navigating life's unbearable losses.

With Grace and Hope,

Pam

BIBLIOGRAPHY

The Forever Grief
James Moore, *When Grief Breaks Your Heart* (Abingdon Press, 1995).
Triggers
Albom Mitch, *For One More Day* (Hachette Books, 2014).
Milestones
Beth Moore, *Feathers from My Nest* (Broadman & Holman, 2001).

Pam McCarty is a mother, grief counselor, and lifelong educator who has spent years walking alongside parents navigating the loss of a child. She leads the Grace for Grief group in her hometown and speaks nationally on bereavement, healing, and hope after loss. Pam holds a master's degree in education and taught at the University of Memphis for thirteen years. Following the death of her daughter, Morgan, she became an advocate for change, helping to pass legislation in Morgan's name and founding the Morgan McCarty Scholarship Foundation. Pam lives in Tennessee with her husband and family.

The Morgan Leah McCarty Scholarship Fund
https://www.morganmemsch.com/
https://pammccarty.com/

Substack: https://substack.com/@pammccarty

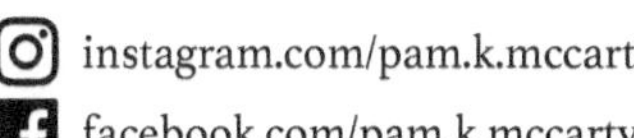

www.ingramcontent.com/pod-product-compliance
Lightning Source LLC
LaVergne TN
LVHW091306150826
845673LV00006B/1556

* 9 7 9 8 9 9 5 0 3 8 0 1 6 *